JASON BLOOMQUIST

NEAR ME

INTRODUCTION

Welcome to 2021, and the new normal in the business world. The way things were, and all your expectations, goals, and business strategies were likely coughed or sneezed right out the window.

Starting and operating a business is more of a courtship resulting in marriage, and this work draws on that theme from start to finish. Time management, exit strategies, formation, processes, checklists, branding, advertising, marketing, web design, social proof, search engine optimization, money, taxes, and franchises easily relate to any successful relationship. If you don't know where you're going in business, or with marriage you'll end up someplace else. This is NOT a get rich quick book that promises four-minute abs or 'fool proof' fads that generate millions overnight.

This work for the average Joe or Jane on main street, who run or want to start a small business from home, or a brick and mortar with a shoestring budget. If you're quick to act, don't refuse change and keep your nest eggs in different baskets you can not only survive, but thrive. This book is about creating a lean and relevant business and executing fundamentals expertly. You don't need a business or law degree to understand this book, everything that may seem complicated on the surface is summarized in simple terms with relatable examples. This book is designed for main street, and work from home hopefuls not multi-faceted conglomerates. Whether you provide a professional service, skilled labor, or sell your wares from a small shop or online, this book is for you.

If you run or want to start a new business home based or brink and mortar in any of the following categories, this book is a **MUST READ.**
Beautician, bookkeeping, audio-video design or installation, blog writing, consulting, carpenter, cleaner, childcare, child proofing, dog walking, pet sitting, pet grooming, ghost or content writing, eldercare, electrician, event planner, food delivery, food trucks, freelancers, graphic design, general contracting, HVAC, hardscaping, home inspection, home organization or decluttering, home staging, in home daycare, interior design, mobile barber or hairdresser, movers and couriers, music lessons, painters, personal training, photographer, plumber, property maintenance, property staging, real estate, transportation, tax preparation, travel agents, tutor and mentors, virtual assistant, voice over artist and readers, web design, wedding coordinator and many many more.

Table of Contents

Chapter 1: Exit Strategy..*6*

Chapter 2: Planning...*21*

Chapter 3: SOP's...*43*

Chapter 4: BAM...*57*

Chapter 5: First Impressions.................................*69*

Chapter 6: Social Proof..*82*

Chapter 7: Marketing Strategies.........................*96*

Chapter 8: Money and Taxes..............................*118*

Chapter 9: Franchises.......................................*145*

Chapter 10: Getting Started..............................*151*

Chapter 1: Exit Strategy

You found what seems to be the love of your life, your true passion. You've flirted with the idea, went through the courtship rituals, and you're thinking about popping the question. You're excited to make the leap and take the first steps down the aisle. The possibilities seem endless! It starts with a honeymoon where the rose-colored sunglasses make everything look better. New ideas are as frequent as the sex. There may be some false starts, awkward moments and times where it seems like it will never end-- both good and bad ways. In hindsight (pun intended), you may realize there are things you shouldn't have done or could have done better. Once the honeymoon ends, the real work begins. The core of a successful business, like marriage is communication, consistency, and being there when you're needed most. This begs the question, is your "marriage" built on convenience or sheer necessity? The expert salesman can convince you everything is a need just like the first date illusion, but buyers' remorse may be just around the corner.

The average consumer needs you or your product to be consistent and reliable. They want it to make their life easier, better and they don't want to have to think too much about it. A perfect match to your skills and passions can fulfill you, prop you up, and make you a better person. Likewise, they can make you insecure, destroy your relationships, and bankrupt you. Sound familiar?

According to the U.S. Bureau of Labor Statistics approximately 20% of new businesses fail during the first two years of being open, 45% during the first five years, and 65% during the first 10 years. Only 25% of new businesses make it to 15 years or more. I wonder how those numbers compare to the national divorce rate? The big question is, are you

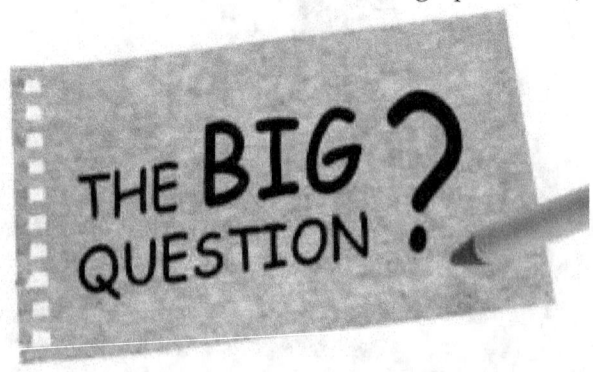

comfortable with those odds?

Are they comfortable with those odds? Before you answer that, think about your family if you have, or want one. Who will rely on your income to survive? Are you willing to roll the dice and risk their future as well?

Owning your own business and working for yourself often is associated with 'freedom' to make your own schedule and rules. As nice as that sounds, you don't reap those benefits in the first few years, or ever if you don't set and stick to guidelines. So, ask yourself: "do I want to own a job, or own a business?" Understanding the difference is not as complicated as you may think. If you're an existing business "owner" consider this: If you stopped working right now, where would your business be in a month, six, a year or more? Would it continue to make profits without you at a rate that supports your lifestyle and budget? You own a job, not a business if it can't function or generate profit without you being involved. If you own a 'job' now and think it's a business, or really want to start a business (not just create a job) you bought the right book.

Before you buy business cards, register with the government, or spend dime on a marketing strategy, re-evaluate your time. It's your most valuable resource, and the only thing you can't get back. Every business is an investment requiring time and money. You need one of the two to start, and both to keep going. You've heard the phrases 'time is money' or 'buying time', but time is irreplaceable. You can't buy yesterday or get a refund if you don't like what you spent it on.

168 Hours

Step ONE is looking at your time and evaluating what it's worth to you **AND** to others. You have 168 hours a week, 24 hours per day just like everyone else. How much of those 168 hours do you want to invest, and how many per day? Decide or determine if your business or idea a side gig (10 hours a week), part time (20 hours a week), full time (40 hours a week), or all in (60+ hours a week)? Draw a line in the sand right now for what you are willing to commit, and where are you taking that time from. [PITFALL] "I'm available and ready 24/7-365 to my customers and clients" is the common theme for new entrepreneurs. "I work when my customers or clients need me!" If that's your mantra, you already lost the 'freedom' and 'flexibility' you thought you got by owning a business, and making your own hours? If you're available whenever your customers need you and you don't draw a line, you don't make your own schedule – they do.

Put your time in perspective; let's assume you sleep seven hours a day (-42) one hour for personal care like bathing (-7), and two hours a day for meals (-14). That leaves you with 105 hours over seven days, or 15 hours a day. Of course, we aren't calculating other things you may want or need to do like having a day off, grocery shopping, medical appointments, commute time or anything you want to do outside of work. If you have or want a family, how much time do they get? Unless you plan on not eating, bathing or sleeping, that time comes from somewhere.

As Stephen Covey says: "Begin with the end in mind." No matter how much time you want to commit, set an end date. Meaning if you're committing 10 or 60+ hours per week, when will you add more or reduce them? What needs to happen to add or reduce hours happen, and how will you measure it? [PITFALL] The 'job owner' answer is always "when I make enough money". The problem with that is you never know how much is enough, and you don't put a value on your time. $50k per year? For what, 10 hours a week or 60+? Setting the premise for your availability is key for your sanity, and the sustainability of your business. Have you ever called a service or business at their listed hours only find they aren't open when you called? Did you wait until they opened and called you back or did you call a different business that performs the same service? Being available AND not available at consistent times is KEY. You may lose customers at first by not being open, but in the long run you are setting the premise to own a business, not a job. If you don't set a premise you may have to answer calls at midnight `for the rest of your life or risk losing customers over time.

- **EXAMPLE:** For some reason I only want *Chic-Fil-et* ™ on Sundays, and they aren't open. But every other day of the week, the drive through line runs on to the highway

When you set your times and are consistently available during them, you become a reliable business and can create milestones and checkpoints. There will be downtime and slow seasons for many businesses, however that is when you schedule business maintenance, payroll, accounting and other necessary non-customer related activities.

Let's bring time back to basics, so you can determine what yours is worth. Before jumping back on to Amazon to buy a fancy 'productivity' day planner or research the newest coolest time tracking app let's not waste and more time or money. Get a blank notebook or a couple sheets of paper and a pencil, copy paper works best because there are no lines. Divide it up in to 35 squares horizontally, five rows down, seven rows across (like a calendar). Write in all the days and numbers for **_last month_**.

- **EXAMPLE:** If It's March 2021, write in February 2021. Later, you can go crazy and search online for a template and print it, but this is about fundamentals, and saving time. You don't need the added temptation to check emails, social media or watch a cat video.

To the best of your knowledge, write down everything you did last month in short form [W] for 'woke up' and [B] for when you went to bed or fell asleep for every day, with the time. Next write in any appointments or pre-existing commitments you had like a doctor appointment, grocery day, laundry day, gym or picking up / dropping off kids at daycare where applicable. If you have a job (employee) or have a business already, write down when you left for work and when you got home.

SIMPLE KEY: [W] Woke Up **[B]** Bed-Time **[A]** Appointment **[J]** Job **[P]** Personal Time **[F]** Family, Fun, Friends **[C]** Commuting.

- _I know this seems simple and ridiculous if you've been running a business but bear with me because you already invested in this book and the point is coming._

It doesn't matter right now _what you're going to do_, what matters is what you did because history repeats itself. You had 24 hours every day, account for them right now. If there were a bunch of holidays and you didn't do what you normally would do because of them, then the question is – will they not exist next year?

Now, how much time do you have available each day based off last month? Meaning, how many hours and which ones can you squeeze in time to work your business? Write down in each little square daily, how many hours you have remaining.

- **EXAMPLE:** Tuesdays (4), Thursdays (4), and Saturdays (4) 8am-Noon.

If you plan on quitting your full-time job to start your business, do you have the funds to cover your personal expenses while it's getting up and running? If not, you may want to start it as a gig or part time, and again, pencil in your deadline to drop full-time job and increase your hours. Right away you should be able to see how much time and which hours each day you could have committed to your business last month. Flip the page in the notebook or grab another sheet of copy paper and project out the next 11 months. Pencil in days you may want off, will close, as well as time blocks for appointments you made and kept.

If you currently run a business, pencil in the hours you spent working with existing customers or clients. Not waiting for the phone to ring, or someone to come through your front door—actual customer engagement. Don't forget to pencil in all holidays, birthdays and time you may want to take a vacation or do something requiring full or multiple days. Want the same day off every week, [X] the day out. Your fantasy football draft may be a major life event for you, or your kids first day of school or graduation. Write everything in including binge watching your favorite show. Sure, right now you may say to yourself "Self, you won't do that thing when the time comes", but you will. [PITFALL] when you first start a business, taking shortcuts with time planning almost guarantees it won't last a year. As John Lennon said, "Life happens when you're busy making other plans".

Avoid the pitfall of 'all day, every day, 24/7-365' because the one time you aren't available, will start the trend of 1. Being unreliable or 2. Taking time from someone or somewhere else and not valuing yours.

Tuesdays, Thursdays, Saturdays 8am-12noon is four hours a day, three days a week = [12 hours a week]. Naturally, you would think just multiply that by 52 because there are 52 weeks in a year. WRONG. Look at the 12-month projection, which birthdays, holidays, special occasions fall on your Tuesday, Thursday or Saturday. Sure, you may say 'I'll work that day' but depending on your business or service, will customers want or need you that day?

- **EXAMPLE:** If your business is dog walking, hair stylist or landscaping do you expect or think new customers or clients are going to call you on Christmas day? Maybe, but is being open and available that day more valuable to you, your family, or the pseudo emergency dog walking scenario?

The most important thing to pencil in your projected calendar is time for yourself, and your family, friends, and significant others. If you don't schedule time for the most important people in your life and stick to it, then your business will suffer. When your business suffers, the perpetual downward spiral will affect the people most important to you.

It's much easier to choose what you want 'now' instead of what you want 'more'. Right now, your planning on running your business and working to make it succeed and that's what you want more. In six months if you don't block out and plan to work that day, the 'more' may be taking a nap. It's easy to say you want a successful business 'more'… this second. Once the honeymoon will be over, and you will want a different 'now'.

If you stopped reading, and grabbed the piece of copy paper, you are way ahead of the game. Many existing business owners will dismiss this simple step until they get to the end of this book but then will have to back track, and they probably won't. That's o.k. because you are already eliminating competition by not being lazy.

Count the Days

How many days are you open for business over the next 12 months? Which days specifically, and how many hours per day? Where is the consistency? Those are your operating hours or open for business hours.

Before we monetize your time, how many hours are you going to work for free to start up? Naturally, starting or restarting takes time—web design, marketing, advertising, testing processes, systems and the binder full of paperwork you'll need to create. If you're a gig  worker, you may budget full time (40hrs) for free for the first 30 days, but when do you need to see a return on investment of this time?

This is your first milestone for your projection.

- Specific days and times you will work over the next 12 months
    o Deadline for working FREE

Monetize your time

Now that you've established **exactly** how many hours you will work, on which days and at which specific times on each day, the next question is "what is your time worth"? Aside from pursing a passion, and creating your own schedule, many entrepreneurs start or go into business to make money or have 'financial freedom'. Whether it's a gig, part-time, full-time or all in, knowing the exact number of hours will allow you to specifically monetize your time, and create an exit strategy.

The everyday Joe or Jane who works for someone else easily can monetize their time. If they are paid by the hour, that is what this time is worth. If you're paid a salary for 40hrs of work per week, simply divide it by 2080. If you've been in business for the last year or more, and this is the reset for you; reverse engineer your calendar (look back 12 months) and count your days times and hours and divide it up by what your net income was.

- **EXAMPLE:** If you're paid $15 an hour, your time is worth $15 an hour. If you're paid a $50k salary for 40hr work weeks / 2080 your time is worth $24.04 per hour. Of course, this doesn't count or include additional perks and benefits you may get through an employer.

Working for someone else, you have that steady income regardless of your level of effectiveness. You can expect regular incremental payments for your time. When you own a business, it pays through performance. If you just show up to your business and do nothing, money isn't likely hitting your bank account. [PITFALL] New business owners, and often existing business owners don't place a specific value on their time. This is the first indicator that determines if you own a job or own a business. Often if they do, they negotiate with themselves this value, or sporadically CHOOSE to work for free when it comes to some tasks, situations or scenarios. [PITFALL] "I'll just keep the profits throughout or at the end of the year". If and when the time comes to expand, or decrease your hours or you end up want to hire a manager, will their salary be "just keep the profits throughout or at the end of the year?" If you don't create a salary or place a value on your time in the very beginning, you will never own a business – you will own a job.

Start with minimum wage, or a flat salary--$15hr for example AND choose to keep the profits at the end of the year or adjust that salary annually. When you place a specific value on your time, it makes it easier to choose what you want more instead of now. It will help keep things in perspective when you chose to work over personal time.

- **EXAMPLE:** Would I rather work four hours on my Birthday for $60, or spend that time with family and friends? Is working another hour for $15 worth missing a kid's ballgame?

When we get to costing and financial projections (proforma) later in this book, you can and may need to adjust your hourly rate. This value or hourly rate is what you must start paying yourself once your 'free work' and start up time ends.

Fold or go All-in

When will you call it quits? Owning a business is exciting, just like getting married. But sometime people just fall out of love. What needs to happen for you to shut it down or pass the reigns, and when? Your first milestone is when you're paying yourself the $15 an hour no matter what, the second is knowing and decided when to hire a manager for your base $15 an hour or shut everything down. When you decide this before you start or "begin with the end in mind" it will prevent you from having a nasty divorce. What needs to happen to keep going in three, six or 12 months? If you don't define what success or failure looks like, you may counterproductively keep going until the damage is irreparable.

Corporate Structure

Think of your shut it down or pass the reigns as a prenuptial agreement. A prenup comes down to who gets what under what circumstance, who is responsible for debt and assets (money). Your business structure is just like a prenup, there are good and bad structures, and ways to move forward without one. Every entity has different rules, some lax with no formality, others with regular reporting, meetings and additional paperwork. Some structures can begin with a handshake or a verbal agreement, other require more paperwork and registration with the  government. During your courtship leading up to your engagement, the things you say and do may be to impress your future spouse. But once you're married you may not be getting breakfast in bed every day. **BEST PRACTICE:** Regardless of the structure you create, write things down, even if you aren't required to.

- **EXAMPLE:** If we have kids, and divorce, then I get custody, for 50% of the time. If you cheat, then the prenup is invalid, and I get everything.

These terms in the business world typically are called an operating agreement. They outline who gets what, when, and how profits are dispersed. Additionally, they dictate who is responsible in the event things don't work out. Like a prenuptial agreement, you don't necessarily know what the future holds. Choosing the wrong business structure, may result in you being personally responsible for everything the business does. **[PITFALL]** Not creating a formal business structure and operating 'under the table'.

In lieu of becoming another boring business book or getting too much into the weeds take note now:

- This is not a legal suggestion or opinion on what you should or shouldn't do. You should consult your government or state's website and/or a lawyer who specializes in corporate law.

There are thousands of books and resources about business structures. A very common question from most entrepreneurs or business owners is "what kind of business should I be, or form?"

Business structures, like the prenuptial agreement comes down to two main points: who is responsible for what, and money (taxes). When you start your business, taxes aren't likely the top-of-mind topic even though they should be. To save you some time most main street businesses operate as a sole proprietor, or form a single member L.L.C. because they require little to no paperwork, and tax filing is easier.

Many people ask: "what's the best state to incorporate in?" The gut shot answer, you'll hear is "Delaware" because of their lack of sales tax among other things. The tax incentives of Delaware are certainly alluring but they may not necessarily be best for you, or your business. Many states incentivize specific business activities with grants, microloans, and limit regulations which may be more beneficial. It comes down to your goal. If your goal is primarily asset protection, Wyoming and Nevada have some of the strongest protections for single member LLC.

- **OPINION:** If you don't want to get lost in the weeds, or don't want to go through the of extra paperwork, just use the state you live in… at first. **WHY:** Once the business is up and running (and profitable), you can re-cross that bridge, sell it to another entity you create in a different state, dissolve it and rebrand, or file to change location. **EXAMPLE:** When you incorporate in a different state you will need a trusted registered agent to handle all paperwork and be available should someone attempt to sue you. If you aren't available, or the agent doesn't notify you, you may have a default judgment levied against you without even knowing. Registered agents cost money, and you're just starting you may not want to spend extra cash on anything until the business becomes profitable.

You can consult a corporate lawyer, firm, use a law freelancer, or the dozens of DIY websites. If you choose to use a DIY website, know you're just paying for convenience because you can easily go to your states website and do the same thing without fees. Ultimately all they do is take the information you submit and send it to your state. You can save the fee, and just go to your state's website, it's not that complicated. Typical business structures summarized:

Sole Proprietor:

A sole proprietorship is a business structure in which "one person owns an unincorporated business by himself or herself," according to the IRS. However, if you're a sole business owner, you're not limited to choosing a sole proprietorship as your business structure. You can elect to be treated as an LLC by the IRS. Establishing a sole proprietorship might have different filing requirements in some states.

- **POPULAR OPINION**: an unincorporated sole proprietor is one of the worst business structures to form, or in many cases 'not' form and you just operate as yourself. **WHY:** You are held personally liable for everything the business does. **EXAMPLE:** If you're a plumber and fix someone pipes, they burst two months after you fix them and they burst, the homeowner can sue you and take your house.

General Partnership:

"A partnership is the relationship existing between two or more persons who join to carry on a trade or business," according to the IRS. Each person contributes money, property, labor or skill, and expects to share in the profits and losses of the business.

Partnerships deal with income taxes in a manner very different from a corporation, for example. A partnership must file an annual information return to report the income, deductions, gains, losses, from its operations. The company does not pay income tax itself. Instead, the partnership "passes through" profits or losses to its partners. As a result, each partner includes his or her share of the partnership's income or loss on his or her personal tax return.

To create a general partnership, you don't usually need to file any organizational documents with the state. Although not legally required, all partnerships should have a written partnership agreement. The partnership agreement can be very helpful if there is ever a dispute among the partners.

- **OPINION:** A general partnership is frequently referred to as the worst type of organization. **WHY:** It functions like a sole proprietor, but the risk is compounded by the number of partners all of which can do anything on behalf of the business without notifying the other partners. **EXAMPLE:** One general partner may sign a multi-year lease for a new location or buy something with business funds and simply quit or leave the partnership. Whoever is left will be on the hook for the lease and have no money to pay for it.

Another form of partnership is a limited partnership. In some states, a limited partnership requires that at least one partner be the general partner, who has full management control of daily functions and is responsible for debts and obligations. A limited partner, typically investors who give up management control for monetary protection, is also required are only liable for the amount invested.

C Corporations

In forming this type of business, prospective shareholders exchange money, property or both, for the corporation's capital stock. A key feature of a corporation is that, for federal income tax purposes, a C Corporation is recognized as a separate taxpaying entity. A corporation conducts business, realizes net income or loss, pays taxes and distributes profits to shareholders.

Another critical feature of C Corporations is how they are taxed. The profit of a corporation is taxed to the corporation when earned, and then is taxed to the shareholders when distributed as dividends, creating a double tax. The corporation does not get a tax deduction when it distributes dividends to shareholders. Shareholders cannot deduct any loss of the corporation.

S Corporations

The principal big difference between a C corporation and a S Corporation is how they are taxed. With an S Corporation, it passes corporate income, losses, deductions and credits through to their shareholders for federal tax purposes. Shareholders of S Corporations report the flow-through of income and losses on their personal tax returns and are assessed tax at their individual income tax rates. This allows S Corporations to avoid double taxation on the corporate income.

- Basically, the S-CORP doesn't pay taxes or deduct losses, whoever gets the profit or losses adds them to their personal tax return. S Corporations are responsible for tax on certain built-in gains and passive income at the entity level.

Other unique traits of S corporations include features such as limitations on who can be shareholders. Allowable shareholders include individuals, certain trusts and estates. Non-allowable shareholders include partnerships, corporations or non-resident alien shareholders. There can also be no more than 100 shareholders, only one class of stock and some corporations are ineligible to be S Corporations, such as certain financial institutions, insurance companies and domestic international sales corporations.

LLC:

Limited Liability Company or LLC, this business structure is the most common among small businesses. An LLC is a business structure regulated by the state, so laws and practices vary from state to state. Owners of an LLC are referred to as members, and there is no maximum as to how many an LLC can have. Also, most states allow for "single-member" LLCs, which have only one owner; and most do not restrict ownership so LLC members can be individuals, corporations, other LLCs and even foreign entities.

For tax purposes, an LLC can be treated a number of ways by the IRS. For example, the IRS can classify your LLC as either a corporation, partnership or as part of the LLC's owner's tax return, depending on elections made by the LLC and the number of members.

- Creating an LLC is like having a child. If your kid did something wrong, you aren't held liable for their actions, to a point.

This is known as the corporate veil but it's not infallible. Because it's a brand-new social security number, they don't have credit or work history. Therefore, getting a loan is typically more difficult and you may have to co-sign or (guarantee) it yourself…which means if you kid doesn't pay you will now. When tax time comes, you can deduct all the qualified expenses on your tax return just like a child and their daycare (business leases, rent and mortgage) and education (training fees) and a slew of other things.

Employer Identification Number (EIN)

Unless you choose to operate as a sole proprietor or general partnership you will need an Employer Identification Number or (EIN). A corporate entity or structure is like creating another person for your business and the EIN is like their Social Security Number. EIN's a free and only take a few minutes to request online.

National American Industry Classification System (NAICS)

A NAICS (pronounced NAKES) Code is the business type within the North American Industry Classification System. The NAICS System was developed for use by Federal Statistical Agencies for the collection, analysis and publication of statistical data related to the US Economy. https://www.census.gov/eos/www/naics/

A NAICS code doesn't cost you anything, but many business documents will require it, and if you ever plan on applying for a business loan you'll need it. Knowing your NAICS code will also help you down the road when you look for tax incentives and grants. Often, you can just search your state name + grants + your NAICS number OR state name + tax + NAICS number and you'll find some info worth looking in to.

- Create a schedule using last month as a baseline
- Project the next 12 months based off that schedule
- Commit to specific times daily based of your TIME goal, 10, 20, 40 or 60+ hours
- Rain or shine stick to those times
- What is your time worth and establish a base rate + profits
- Identify where you want the business in a month, six, twelve, two and five years.
- Make milestones to assess your progress
- Write everything on paper in pencil, you can change things and things will change
- Write a business prenuptial agreement, what needs to happen to call it quits, or expand
- Business Structures are like prenuptial agreements – who gets what, when and who is or isn't responsible.
- Most new or main street small businesses incorporate as a single member LLC
- NAICS Code: a business type identifier used by Federal Statistical Agencies
- EIN is your businesses social security number

Chapter 2: Planning

You popped the question, and you're getting engaged. Before you happily walk down the aisle and say 'I Do' where do you see this relationship in five years? Do you want kids, how many? Public or private school? Rent a luxury apartment in the city, or buy a house in the suburbs? The biggest question is why? Why do you want these things, and how do you PLAN on paying for them? Many start-ups, business owners and wannabe entrepreneurs struggle with writing a business plan, or they struggle with the different elements of the plan. The main reason for this struggle, and why businesses fail is twofold. 1. They confuse a plan with the model. 2. Start-ups and businesses fail to write everything down, and if they do, they do it once and never review it.

A business plan is simply WHAT you 'plan' to do as a general concept, the 'model' is the nitty gritty HOW you're going to do it. Writing a business plan is necessary if you want to be successful over the long term. Saying "I want to open a business" and throwing money at it doesn't work if you don't have a written plan. Many wannabe entrepreneurs don't write out a plan because they feel their idea is gold, or it's a secret recipe for success only they can know. Fortunately for you, they end up being the bulk of the statistics in the new business failure rate.

Some people find writing a business plan as daunting and tedious because they don't have adequate writing skills to make it look good. A business plan is yours and doesn't need to have complicated academic jargon or terms. It is for you to understand, and you can always change the simple words to what's taught in business school or make it look fancy.

If you don't overcomplicate things, you can write a business plan in about an hour. If you currently own or run a business this exercise will help you trim the fat and increase focus on your core products and services. Unless you have a secret benefactor or tons of cash on hand, re-writing, evaluating, and modifying a business plan regularly is essential. It's a living document, and you should review and update it annually at a minimum to stay in line with market conditions and the tax map. Should you ever need or seek investors, loans, or additional capital you will need a plan before anyone serious AND capable will entertain your idea.

Within any good business plan there are key elements and components depending on your business type or industry. Some industries may require more detail for specific elements, but the basic premise is the same. This section covers each element of a business PLAN with examples followed by blank space so the reader to write in their idea as they follow along. The business model which are the processes, checklists, and detailed descriptions follow in the chapters after.

Typical elements of a business plan: value proposition, market opportunity, competitive environment, competitive advantage, market strategy, organizational development, management team, and revenue model. If you're new to business, don't have an MBA, and don't want to spend tens of thousands of dollars on taking courses this exercise will simplify the whole structure. Business plans come down to simple questions and answers regardless if you want to use the academic terms or not.

1. What do you do, and why? (Core products and services / Value proposition)
2. Who is it for? (Customer, Market opportunity)
3. Who does it now? (Competition)
4. How are you better? (Competitive Advantage/Value Proposition)
5. How you find customers (Marketing)
6. Who's in charge (Ownership/Management/Key Members)
7. How much will it cost and how much will you make in the short, mid and long term (Proforma, revenue model)

Again, the business plan is what you want to do, the model is how you do it. The plan should be reviewed annually, the model should be reviewed quarterly, when the market changes or with the introduction of a new product or service. Grab your notebook and pencil, and you can generate your plan in the simplest form as your read along. The specifics, numbers and detail are covered in later chapters and will take more time and research so leave some blank space so you can refer back and write in notes or ideas as they come.

Core Products, Services & Value Proposition

What do you do and why? Two years ago, if you went to any fast-food joint or restaurant you may have seen hundreds of options, combinations and menu items. If you haven't noticed in the last year many have leaned out their menu to the core products they are known for or have the biggest profit margin. These include all the big burger brands, and they've been around for decades and are worth millions if not billions of dollars. The businesses that survived and thrived quickly adapted to the changing environment but stuck with their core products and services and didn't over complicate things.

One Word:

What is your business in as few words as possible, think 1-3 words as a concept?

- **EXAMPLES:** Café, bar, cleaner, hair salon, travel agent, life coach, daycare, pet groomer, landscaper, graphic designer, photographer etc.

Now write whatever your business type is in GIANT letters in the middle of your copy paper and put a big circle around it. This is what you do, sell, or the service you intend to provide. Don't over complicate it right now, we will get there, and this is for you not a customer. It's not necessary to say gourmet vegan café with an eco-friendly bohemian twist.

CLEANER

What Do You Do or Sell?

What are your core products or services? In as few words as possible, what do you provide or sell? Cleaner can mean many things, so the more specific the better.

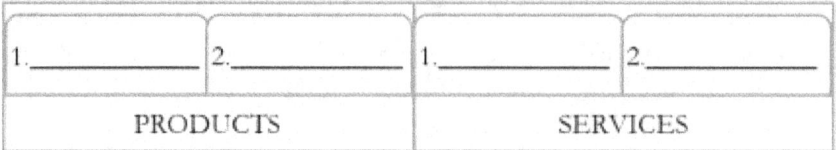

1._____	2._____	1._____	2._____
PRODUCTS		SERVICES	

- **EXAMPLE:** Cleaner can be selling cleaning products like soap, or cleaning things for people with soap. If you say 'Gourmet Italian food' you're already complicating it. Customers aren't going to see this, so say "pizza" and "pasta". More specifically, you should say Made to Order (MTO)-- "MTO Pizza" or "MTO Pasta" unless you are selling raw ingredients or premade so consumers can make their own.

Thus far using cleaner as the example you could say: "I sell cleaning products like soap and polish" OR "I clean houses and storage units".

Why

The next and key question is—why? Meaning: why do what you do, OR why do you sell what you sell? Of course, you do it to make money but put yourself in your customers shoes, why do they want or need what you do or sell? For now, you don't need a thought-provoking quixotic mission statement to save the world, keep it simple and easy for YOU and then go back and make it fancy for lenders if you need to.

- **EXAMPLE:** I sell cleaning supplies because people are dirty. I clean houses because people are lazy.

Selling it or using it?

WHY: People are dirty and lazy

CLEANER

1	2	1	2
PRODUCTS		SERVICES	

Who is it for?

Think back to before you got 'engaged' or when you were dating. What were you looking in a potential spouse? What characteristics are you attracted to and what would stand out? What does that person look like, and where are you most likely to find them? If health and fitness were a top priority are you more likely to find your soul mate at a gym, or a pie eating contest?

Market opportunity often is confused or combined with market strategy and reach. Market opportunity can be thin sliced in to three specific categories: 1. Who is your potential customer 2. Where are they 3. Is the product or service needed? For your business plan, it is about overall numbers within a defined area. Your 'ideal customer, or persona is discussed later'.

Your market opportunity can be broken down for your core products or services.

Are you selling industrial grease cleaner for car engines or hand soap for grand mom? Are you cleaning office buildings, or houses for hoarders? In other words, are you selling or providing products or services to businesses (B2B) OR products and services to consumers (B2C)? Of course, you can do both, but who is your primary focus initially or is there a percentage of each? 25% B2B and 75% B2C? Now, how many potential customers do you have within your service area?

- **EXAMPLE 1:** If you core products are soap and furniture polish what percentage soap will be for businesses and what percentage for home?
- **EXAMPLE 2:** If your cleaning offices, where?
  - Town, post codes, state, country, internationally?
- **EXAMPLE 3:** How many offices are within that area?

Of course, you probably think everyone can benefit from your product or service. However, your market opportunity not only includes who can benefit, but who has the means, desire, and is likely to be interested.

- **EXAMPLE:** If you sell engagement rings with a starting price of $10,000 everyone may want one, but not everyone has that income level to afford it. Couples already married won't likely be interested in an engagement ring. Ultimately who buys engagement rings— men or women…MOST of the time?

If you are selling a tangible product; [selling soap online] that may be nationally or internationally—are there places you wouldn't or can't ship? If your cleaning an office building, which areas or postcodes will you travel to?

- **SCENARIO:** If you are in New York, and someone contacts you from California to clean their house are you hopping on a plane and going—realistically?

Who else does or sells it?

You're in a cocktail or piano bar, maybe a nightclub. There are dozens of people who catch your eye and fit the bill on the surface for what you want in a potential spouse. Who else is eyeing them up, and who are they checking out?

Market analysis is usually what stumps people when it comes to creating your business plan and strategy. Who else does what you do in your target area? They may not provide the exact same services or sell the same products, but before you open up who solves the same problem right now?

Our example is "cleaner". Go on your favorite search engine and search that word "near me" you can add your zip code for better results.

- **EXAMPLE:** "cleaner near me 90210" or "cleaner near 90210".

You will want to look at the map view if available and avoid 'sponsored' posts unless they are local to you. Take note, write down or screen shot the top five results. Too many results, or too much competition? If your "I am" is too general, you may get completely unrelated results. Cleaner would garner multiple results like dry cleaner, carpet cleaner maybe even mold removal or remediation experts.

This is Search Engine Optimization (SEO) at work for other companies. Fine tune your search and your main words to who you want to service. If you were a customer, what words would you search for generally to find a service like yours? Don't use a company name because ultimately if no-one knows the company name, or it has bad SEO it won't pop up without exact matches and even then, it still may not be the top result. "Commercial window cleaner near me", "House Cleaner near 90210", "Maid service near Beverly Hills" will all be more effective. If you are still determining your focus or deciding between B2B or B2C this exercise will help identify if there is a need. If the top 20 results show all residential, but few commercial – maybe consider specializing in commercial. Add the top three best results for B2B and B2C based off the number of reviews and search ranking— reviews are more important than ranking. If a competitor is #1 but has no reviews, it doesn't mean they are the best, it just means they have the best SEO.

How are you better?

I'm better looking than her, that guy looks like a meathead. He is way too drunk to be on the dance floor, she has toilet paper stuck to her heal. As you look for your ideal partner, you subconsciously size up the competition, or sometimes just blatantly say what you're thinking. Though it's never a good idea to say something bad about the competition, you may still think it.

Competitive advantage is how are you different, but more importantly how are you better and why should someone use you or your product over someone else. Now you know who the potential competition is, fine tune it. Our example showed five cleaning services, what do you and they specialize in? If you are focused on B2B do the top five focus on B2B, or B2C etc.

Check out their websites and reviews. What is their pricing model or structure, what do their customers say good and bad about them? What is their competitive advantage or what do they claim to do better than all the competition? Price, speed, quality, service, simplicity etc.?

If you see thousands of 5-star reviews saying they are the best house cleaners on the planet, and their pricing structure according to their website is way lower than yours, they are fast and do next or same day appointments then you have your work cut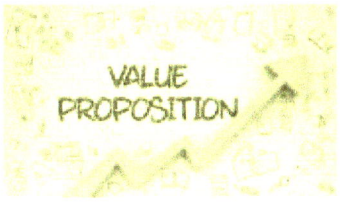

out for you. You will need to find what you do better, and why people should use you instead…Or maybe change your perspective and focus on commercial clients.

Just because there may be a lot of competition doesn't mean your business will fail, there may be a tremendous amount of competition because there is a huge need. Your competitive advantage will need to quickly and clearly tell people why you are better. If you can't say who you are, what you do and why your better in a tweet, you are behind the power curve.

The reality is customers want everything and they want it for free. Many new businesses say they will provide better service, but when your brand is new you may not have reviews suggesting great service so that claim falls on deaf ears. The starting point for competitive advantage is a triangle with three categories, speed, quality and price. When you prioritize the top two, you likely won't get the third. Meaning, if you want high quality fast, it won't

be cheap. If you want it fast and cheap, you may sacrifice quality. Lastly, if you want high quality cheap, it won't be fast. Your core products or services will need to beat the competition in at least two out of three. Service matters, but if you are losing on all three categories improve a process to be more competitive. If you can't, you won't win.

- **EXAMPLE:** If you were charged with murder, and you could choose between two attorneys. Both are the same price and speed; one is a complete jerk but has a 90% chance of getting you off. The other is delightful and but has a 40% chance of getting you off— who would you pick? If you are competitive in at least two of the three categories (fast and inexpensive), focus on improving processes to increase quality.

The next two and most important factors in competitive advantage are service and simplicity. In 2021, service has taken a back seat to simplicity across many industries. A decade ago, if someone suggested people would buy cars without a test drive and learning about all the features and benefits first through a qualified salesperson you may think they were crazy. Today, you can buy a car from a vending machine, or order it online and have it delivered to your door – no salesperson needed. Consumers focus on the triangle points before your service quality if they don't know you.

High quality service in a restaurant is irrelevant if consumers can't eat in. They may still order from you if it's simple and easy. One click buying or fast responses to question is a key competitive advantage. If a customer sees your triangle, how many steps are required to engage and hire you?

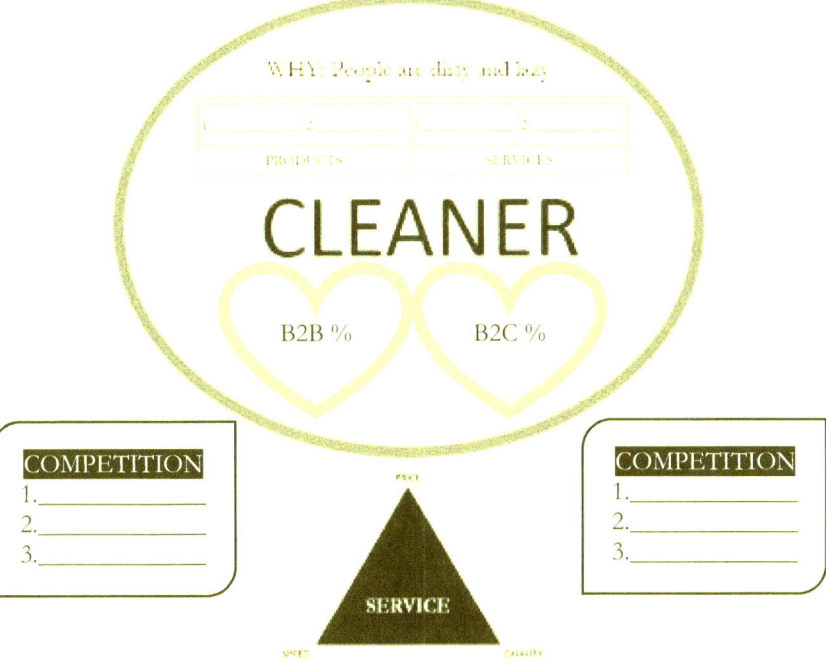

How will you talk to or engage customers?

"Hey Bartender, do you see that red head over there? I'd like to buy them a drink." How will you find, reach, and engage customers?

Nearly every new entrepreneur, and many existing businesses think this is easy. Throw together a website, social media, buy business cards, use word of mouth and referrals. If you have a bigger budget, maybe your buying commercial time, a billboard, radio ad, car wrap, mass mailing flyers, email marketing and buying lists.

All these things may work in one way or another if used correctly and consistently. When creating your plan, choose your top 5 and create a pro-con list weighting time, money and effectiveness. Create a line item for your plan with the cost (both time and money), frequency, reach, per product or service.

- **EXAMPLE:** I will mass email my client base of 10k a custom newsletter once a month about my soap. It will take me 1 hour ($15) to create and email.
- **EXAMPLE:** I will post on my social media a new video weekly using my soap for my 2k followers. Creating the video and comment follow ups will take me 1hr a week or 4hrs a month ($60).
- **EXAMPLE:** I will rent a billboard with a 50k vehicle per day (VPD) exposure for my soap. It will cost $1,200 per month and $500 for a one-time design fee.

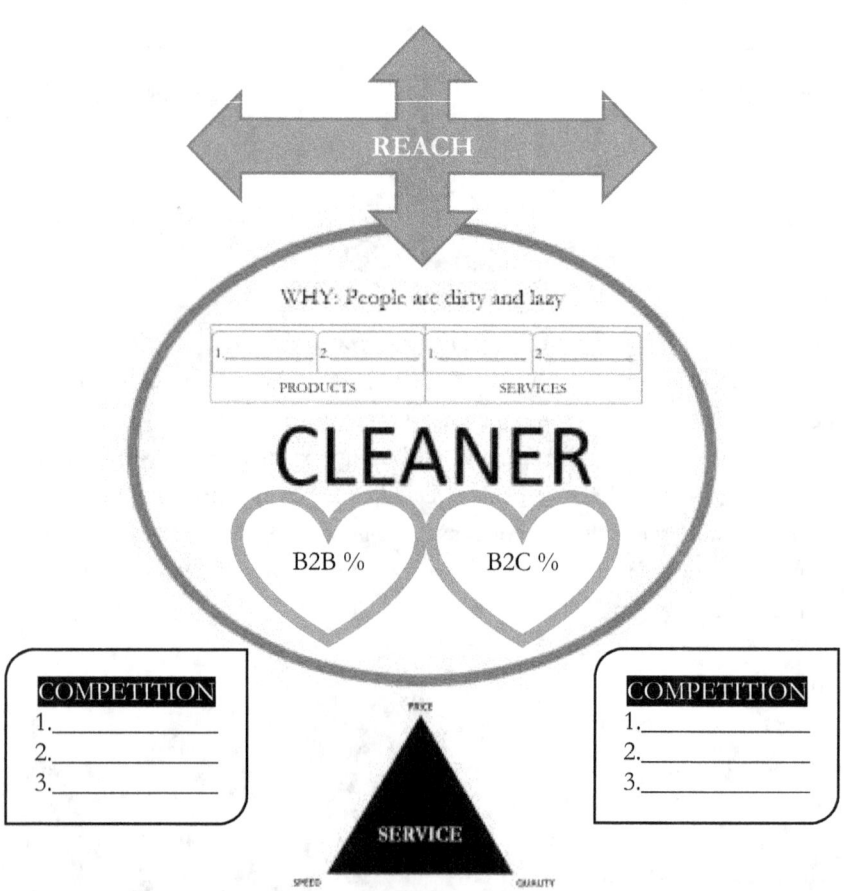

Who will help you?

If you struck out at the bar, maybe you needed a wingman? If you had a wingman who ran interference on the competition or introduced you could have saved time and sent far less drinks across the bar. Every business has key members, whether they are owners, advisors, employees or not. Identify your wingmen, and what they bring to the table. They be owners, managers, financiers, members, mentors, partners and even influencers. Who decides on the direction of the company and business? The individuals matter quite a bit to lenders if you're looking to borrow money at some point, but also for processes and reach. When submitting for a business loan, many lenders want to know who is on your team that will help it be successful, but also who will be liable if things don't work out.

The starting point for key members is their resume and experience. If

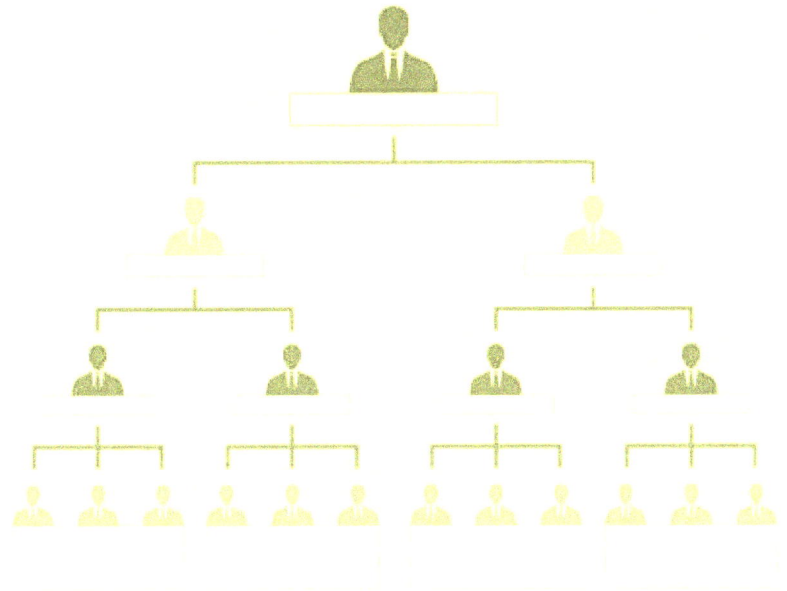

you're business is legal consulting, you probably need some lawyers on the team. If your business is supply chain or shipping, having a member or manager that has experience in this will both increase credibility, but also improve processes. Ultimately, these are the individuals who have a voice **AND/OR** the authority, to influence decisions for the company's direction in the short and long term.

Influencers can also be a key role, and many larger businesses pay for movie stars, athletes, and other spokesman to support the brand. If your business is selling soccer balls, and your best friends with Cristiano Reynaldo that would be important to add. These members or owners are key players or partners in your business, whether they are compensated or not. They are your board of directors and advisors, even if the final decisions lie with you.

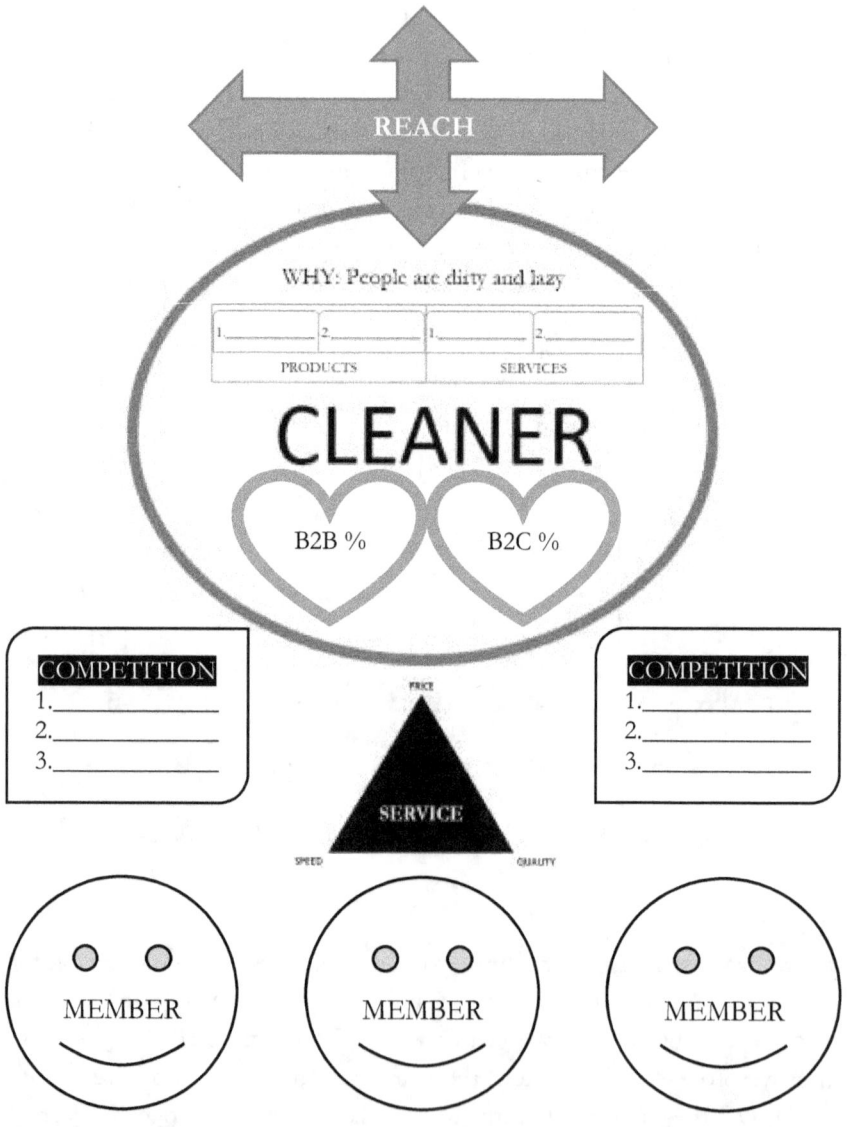

How much will it cost, and how much will you make?

Did you buy a new outfit before going out? Did you take a taxi or uber to get to the night club? Is there a cover charge? How many drinks did you buy for yourself and for others? How often are you going to the bar in search of love on average per month? Some people aren't good at math, and that's O.K. Costing out a business is fun for some people, if you're a coupon cutter or savvy shopper you may enjoy it.

Costing out a small business just requires basic math. Anything complex, there is probably an APP or calculator for it. More complex math and taxes are covered later, and you can always hire an accountant. **[PITFALL]** many new businesses neglect to cost out EVERYTHING and just focus on the big things.

Break Expenses Down

Can you eat a six-foot-long hoagie? Maybe, but not usually in one sitting. You have to cut it up into smaller pieces otherwise it will fall apart the second you start. Costing out a business is broken down into two elements revenue and expenses, which ultimately is profit and losses. A proforma, or cost projection is simply a long-term forecast of your revenue and expenses that result in your profit and losses. The easy way to cost out a business is to create a list of every expense you will incur in one year. Some items may be annual, quarterly, monthly, bi-weekly, weekly or daily. Look back at your pseudo calendar created in chapter one. For every expense you will incur in the next 12 months, add a [$] on the day it will be incurred, and the amount. Start with your time. If you are committing to part time hours: four hours a day ($15hr) five days a week and you blocked out that time on your calendar add [-$60] on each day you will work. Other common items to consider:

- Rent, lease, mortgage
- Marketing
- Licenses, insurance and permits
- Property and equipment expenses
- Cost of Goods Sold (COGS)
- Utilities, technology and communications

By no means is this an all-inclusive list, just the starting point. A more comprehensive checklist is available in Chapter 10.

Cost Per Day

Once you have a list of your total expenses for a year, look back at your calendar and how many days you will be open. NOT how many days in the year, unless you are open every single day including holidays. Divide the total annual expense by the number of days you will be open. Remember, some expense items will be once a year, month, week or day—you should still calculate it as a cost per day.

- **EXAMPLE:** Annual expense is $18,750 and you are open 250 days in one year. You will need to generate $75 per day to break even.

Tangible Products

Selling a physical or tangible product is easier to cost out. The 3 key factors for tangible products to consider:

1. Are disposable or one-time use, like a sandwich
2. Are they one off larger purchases, like a table?
3. Are they products that may need service after sale like a photo copier? This is important because you may sell multiple sandwiches to the same person in any given year, but the chances of the same person buying a table or photo copier daily is far less likely. The elements to consider with businesses who sell a tangible product often is referred to as COGS or Cost of Goods Sold. COGS formula is the cost of acquiring or manufacturing the products that a company sells during a period, so the only costs included in the measure are those that are directly tied to the production of the products. These costs include labor, materials, and manufacturing overhead (waste).

- **EXAMPLE:** If you run a catering business out of your home focusing on hamburgers your COGS would be meat, buns, cheese, lettuce etc. (materials). Time to cook everything (labor) and all the burgers and buns you burned or were moldy when you opened the bag (overhead or waste).

These items should be listed on your proforma or business cost projection. Now, how many burgers to you need to sell per day to break even? With our example of $75 per day needed to break even (you added your time value) you would need to sell 25 burgers at $3 each per day. If you know some days you won't sell any burgers, you may need to sell more on other days, or increase the cost per burger.

Services

When you sell a service, time savings, skills, labor, knowledge and experience are your product. Time is expensive and irreplaceable; many people pay to save time, but it comes down to what their time is worth AND yours. People also pay for convenience, is what you provide easy and convenient? Lastly, people pay for knowledge and skills. Are you providing knowledge or skills that will make things easier or better for them?

Professional services in the past primarily worked on a billable hour schedule, like lawyers, accountants, and personal trainers. However, in the digital age, many professional service providers have modified their billing schedules to flat fees for the most common services. Many professional service providers have abandoned the most basic services in general due to the work not being worth their time, or unwillingness to compete for smaller sales. These services have been replaced and automated for far less within a few clicks on the internet.

Just because you can do something yourself, doesn't mean you should and that is a key in your competitive advantage if you sell a service. ***Getting that point across to a customer isn't always the easiest thing.*** If you've ever lost a sale over a few dollars because a potential client used an automated service or website instead of a pro (like you), you probably 'hoped' secretly or maybe screamed "I hope you get screwed over by the internet".

What's your time worth?

So, what is your time worth? For professionals and professional services, it's always a difficult question. First determine if you want to charge flat fees, the hourly billing method, or a combination of both. If you are brand new to selling yourself, which is what you're doing the next most important factor is your time commitment. If this is a side gig, you may not worry as much about revenue whereas if the is full time or all in it may be your lifeline.

Knowing how much you need to make to cover all your business expenses (including your time) AND your personal expenses is key.

Most consumers don't care if you can pay your bills or not, they care about paying their bills, I know, sad but true. To initially cost this out, look back at your initial goal of time. Take a look at or make a personal budget. How much do you need to make per hour or day for this business venture to be worth it? If you can't pay your bills, business and/or personal, the business may not survive very long even if you have the best everything.

How many flat rate services or hours do you need to bill per day, week or month? If you intend on charging a flat rate for specific services, you will still want to turn or convert them into an hourly value.

- **EXAMPLE:** If you're a landscaper and charge a $50 flat rate to cut someone's lawn and it requires two hours, your hourly is $25 per hour.

When you convert flat rates into hourly expenses, you can easily identify cost overruns or whether a job is worth taking on. With our $50 flat rate to cut a lawn, you may find some lawns take more than two hours, or the commute distance is twice as far and therefore it's decreasing the hourly rate.

Do you have specialized skills or knowledge? If so, are those skills or knowledge required for the work you are performing? If not, they may not be worth much in the eyes of a consumer.

- **EXAMPLE:** A web designer with a degree in biology probably isn't worth more than one without one. If the website you're designing is science based, then maybe.

If you sell or perform a service like a general contractor or plumber, those are specialized skills. The key to higher flat rates or billable hours is social proof (discussed in Chapter 6). Even though plumbers in your area may get $150 an hour, if you're brand new you may have to start lower for a few jobs based off your value proposition and competitive advantage. All things equal, if no-one has reviewed your business, you may simply lose the job to someone who has 50 5* reviews.

- **EXAMPLE:** If 10 landscapers said they would cut my grass for $50, and you came by and said $300 it's not likely I'll hire you even if you have a PhD in math, because the math doesn't add up.
- To determine your service cost or hourly rate, take your total annual expenses, divided by the number of days you intend on working from chapter one. Divide the amount by the number of hours you intend on working. This will be your break-even baseline.

SCENARIO:
- Annual expense not including your salary: $10,000
- Your (or future manager) hourly rate: $15hr
- Number of hours per day: 5
- Number of days you will work or be open: 200
- 15hr x 5 hrs x 200 days = $15,000 + $10,000 annual expenses = $25,000
- $25,000 / 200 days = $125 a day or $25-hour minimum service cost to break even. Anything above this will be profit you keep.

If you need additional help with a business plan there are many software programs that will walk you through the steps. www.liveplan.com is an excellent cost-effective solution, at about $20 a month with a generous free trial program.

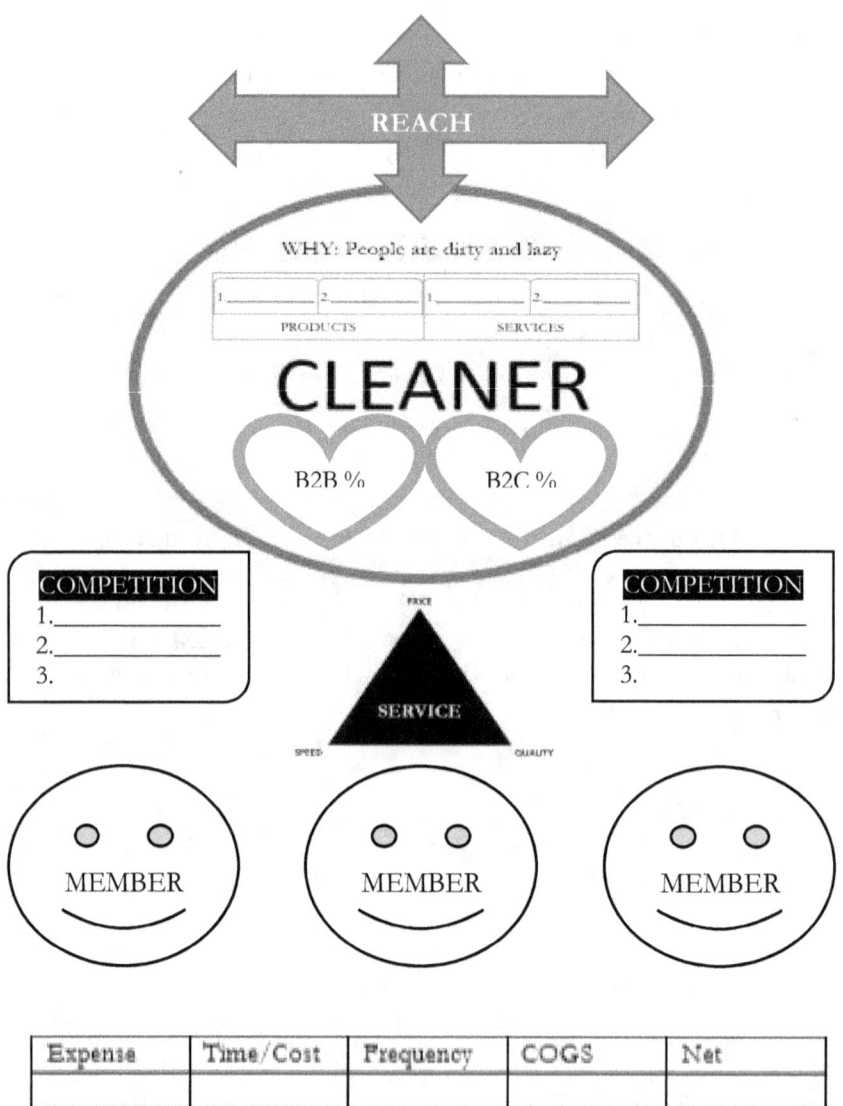

1. What do you do, and why? (Core Products/Competitive Advantage)
2. Who is it for? (Customer, Market opportunity,)
3. Who does it now? (Competition)
4. How are you better? (Competitive Advantage/Value Proposition)
5. How will you find and talk to customers? (Marketing/Reach)
6. Who oversees or owns the business (Ownership/Management/Key Members)
7. How much will it cost you, and how much will you earn--over time (Proforma, cost prospective, revenue model)

Once you have a basic business plan outline, it's time to create standard operating procedures (SOP's) and your business model.

Chapter 3: SOP's

Congratulations! You've found someone who complements you in every way. They have the same goals and aspirations in life, and you just moved in together. Now the real work begins to stay connected, flaws and all. You both have lives and goals, but they intersect at the right places and times, and you couldn't be happier. Who does the grocery shopping, walks the dog, cooks, cleans, washes the laundry and gets control of the remote?

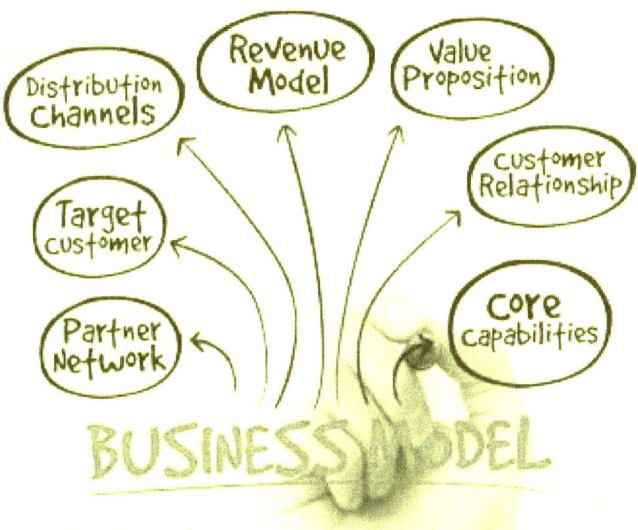

Every business, small, medium, large, brick and mortar, home-based, one or 1000 employees is a collection of systems and processes. Buzz words, logo's, high-rise buildings and fancy websites mean nothing if you don't have a system to provide a product or service to a customer. This section is about processes, checklists and modeling your business.

Like your prenuptial agreement, a business model is the compilation of 'If-then-what' systems and scenarios. If you cook dinner, I will do the dishes—while I'm doing the dishes, you walk the dog and I'll throw a load of laundry in. Once you have your plan and outline, break each element in to a process with a checklist. The combined list of processes and checklist is called your Standard Operating Procedures (SOP). In a relationship, they are your habits and routines for daily life.

Businesses start with an idea, or a need to solve a problem. Many new businesses don't evolve around new ideas or even new problems. Often, they are old idea's repackaged and optimized for better efficiency. Businesses that last throughout time evolve and improve systems, processes and checklists to maximize efficiency. You probably know what an employee handbook is. Not only does it contain standards and rules for how an employee should act or present themselves to customers, they include processes and checklists. Depending on the size of the business, there is likely a process and checklist for someone on "how and when" to update that employee handbook!

Before getting in depth with processes and checklists, a quick reminder. Your time is the only thing you can't get back, so wasting it trying to figure out what to do is why you create a checklist or a process. Additionally, if you are all in working your business 60+ hours a week they will allow you to take a break. Depending on how good they are, you may be able to turn that 60+ hours to less than 10 and earn the same amount.

When you think about a process, think of a fast-food restaurant. There is a system in place to get you in the door, accept your order, cooking and constructing your burger, wrapping and packaging, then delivering it to you in less than a specific amount of time. That fast food restaurant has the

processes so specific, that the whole transaction is complete in about two minutes. This is why they can sell that hamburger for only 99 cents. This doesn't mean it's the best burger, you can probably cook a better one. It is however consistent, fast, inexpensive and available whenever you want it. The amount of time for you to shop for ingredients, prepare, cook and clean up afterward is worth more to you than the quality of the burger—so you buy them.

Beyond the burger, there are processes on how to get more raw meat, buns and other ingredients through dozens of supply chains. There are checklists and inventories to ensure accuracy and quality standards. It you eat the burger or get the wrong order, they have another process on how to refund, replace or fix your customer experience. If you have a bad experience, their receipt has a survey and contact information to complain.

Design or redesign processes and checklists for every element or function within your business. A process is "If this happen, I'll do this" or a "if, then, what" system. Think back to the prenuptial agreement: "If we divorce and we have kids, then I get custody, for 50% of the time. If you cheat, then the prenup is invalid, and I get everything." They are simple flow charts with no more than ten steps. Each step can and should have a simple checklist written with steps and short bullet points. The bullet points can include scripts, questions to ask, and

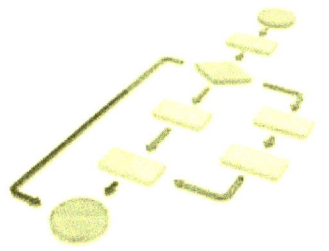

actions to take that assist in moving to the next step. An effective workflow and process checklist should be so simple that if you needed help with a task, you could simply hand it to someone with no experience and they can execute.

- **EXAMPLE:** If you ever purchased something from the Swedish furniture giant IKEA™ the included instructions are the process, and each step is a checklist. Everything they sell regardless if there is only one step has a process checklist—even their boxes instruct on which side to open before accessing the process checklist. Although the one step may be obvious to 99% of customers the checklist prevents the 1% from calling a customer service agent and thereby increasing the item cost via a customer service agent.

Processes and checklists often require manual labor or hands on tasks when you first start or restart your business. You may know every process forward and backwards but writing it down is how you transition from owning a job to owning a business. You may have heard of the sales funnel or pipeline, if so that's a start, but that's only one workflow process. You can and should have a process and supporting checklist for every aspect of your business. They will eliminate confusion, create consistency, trust and save time.

Have you ever called a business or organization with a question, and the individual who answered the phone said, "I'm not sure, let me check"? If you operate an existing business, have you or a staff member ever said it? How much time was required to find the answer? Seconds, minutes, a call back? Whatever the cost in time, there probably is a process or checklist that could have avoided that hold, however brief. If you or the caller are existing customers who already made the purchase, you may stay on the line or wait for the call back. What if it's a lead or potential new client, and you need to research and call back later? That's a failure in a process which may lead the potential client to call a competitor who has the answers on hand and can move them through the pipeline immediately. Not only is it a lost sale, but it's wasted money on the marketing and advertising you spent to get them to call in the first place.

Key Performance Indicators (KPI)

If you're always late for dinner, your new significant other may stop cooking. Regardless of the process or checklist, you must measure its effectiveness and whether it can be improved and sometime whether it's needed at all. A key performance indicator (KPI) is the measurement tool you create 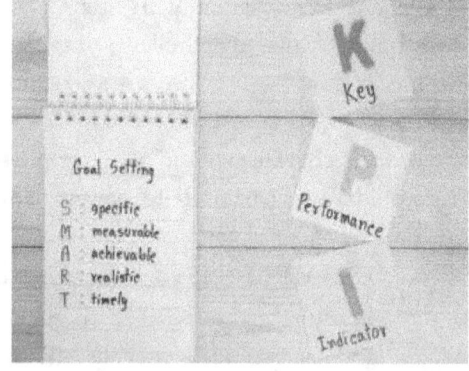 and use to constantly assess efficiency. Often KPI's are time delineated, but not always.

- **EXAMPLE:** The drive through at your burger joint likely has a time delineated KPI. Once the order is place, the preparation process begins, and by the time you reach the window the teller is checking your receipt (checklist of what should be inside the bag) taking your payment, then handing you your food. If you've ever worked in fast food, or went in and looked at the window, you may have seen the actual clock.

KPI's are used in nearly every aspect of business, marketing and advertising are huge ones. Not all KPI's measure speed, sometimes they are used to assess periods of time. "Call within the next ten minutes for a bonus deal". A marketing promo code you see on TV for a pillow is measuring the effectiveness of the advertisement. You may have seen the same commercial at different times in the day for the same product, but the promo code is slightly different.

- **EXAMPLE:** When the pillow ad runs at noon, the promo code may be [TV12]. If it shows up again at 10pm, it may be [TV10]. This is the business or advertiser assessing which time slot results in more sales.

You should have KPI's for every milestone in your business supported by the process to achieve it, and a checklist to complete steps in the process. Successful small businesses review and update their business model and functions regularly to assess KPI's to ensure they're on track. Big business and publicly traded companies are required by law to provide updates quarterly on earnings which are the results of KPI's. Your business model is a living, breathing collection of systems, tasks and checklists that measure your performance. **[PITFALL]** Many small businesses neglect to review their model until times are tough or need a loan. Unfortunately, that often is too late, because lenders don't want to invest in a system that doesn't work or isn't profitable. Whenever you add a new product, service or expand your market a quick update to you model will ensure you grow consistently.

Typical process checklists every business should have:

- Marketing and advertising, getting customers in the pipeline.
  - o How you intend on reaching new customers whether it's a complex marketing plan and strategy, handing out business cards, cold calling, a commercial, billboard, social media targeting or otherwise. Each of these streams should have an associated process and checklist. How you will do it, when you will do it, and how it's measured. Think back to your schedule and projected 12-month calendar—which days and times will you do these functions?
- Inbound leads: phone, web, in person.

o Assume your marketing works, and a new client reaches out to you for your product or service, now what? Have a specific process and checklist for each type of new client contact. In the long run, inbound or new leads will be categorized or prioritize based off a system you create that will identify the level of interest or potential for buying. If you operate a brick-and-mortar location, a new lead who walks in your front door likely is more serious than a web inquiry who didn't leave a phone number. Scripts, qualification questions, consumer profile creation are often associated with inbound leads.

- Outbound communication: phone, web, email etc.
  o After receiving and qualifying the new inquiry, what's the next step? An email to confirm you understand the problem. A follow up call to build more rapport or clarify the need? A quote or invoice? An appointment confirmation or schedule delivery? Do you call to confirm receipt of invoice or quote? Your outbound communication is to keep a client in the pipeline or move them to the next step. Maybe the next step is to start over and requalify.

- Payment processing, payment refunds, disputes and modifications.
  o Each of these items will need a written process and checklist. Does the customer agree to the terms and conditions and want the product or service—do they need to sign something? How will you take the payment? What if the payment method is denied by their bank? What if the payment is accepted, but the client disputes the charge at a later date? What if the client finds the same product for less, and you are price matching?

- Sending, cancelling or modifying an invoice or purchase.
  o If you send an invoice with a buying window, what do you do if that window closes? If the price no-longer valid, what do you do next? Do you need to cancel the invoice and send a new one, or modify the existing one?

- Hiring, firing, performance reviews, disciplinary actions for employees, contractors, freelancers and vendors.

- o Each process should have a checklist for when you need assess your KPI's regarding internal operations, staff, and vendors. Are you getting bigger and need help? Do you need to downsize to cut expenses? Are employees or vendors meeting, exceeding or missing the target goals— what do you do?
- Asking for referrals and reviews, responding to referrals and reviews.
  - o Perhaps one of the most important, but least followed through process for new businesses. Getting reviews and asking for social proof. What if every five start review you got lead to five new leads? Following up with happy customers will save you exponential time and money for nearly every process. A review that states what you did in different scenarios may remove the question when you are qualifying. Reviews and referrals will save marketing and advertising dollars.
- Service after sales and constant contact.
  - o After a client purchases your service or product, it's not a done deal. Even though you may not be selling them another table in the near future, do they need a lamp? If they purchased a service or product that requires maintenance or regular service, what is the process to schedule and perform those services?
- Ordering supplies, products for sale, distribution, manufacturing, and maintenance of systems, equipment and processes.
  - o If a client is standing in front of you to sign their contract and the printer jams, what do you do? What if there is a huge line and the phones are ringing? What if you run out of paper, or the toner is low? Can you sell your hamburgers if you run out of buns? These things happen, and often result in loss of customers or wasting time and money. If you ran out of buns, do you head to the grocery store and buy what's available? Will that now affect your profit margin, and did you budget an hour away from the business? Regular maintenance, or lack thereof results in

cost overruns. This is why popular option is businesses cost twice as much as you project in the first year.

Creating process guides and checklists will decrease wasted time and increase the value of yours in the long run.

- **EXAMPLE:** If a new client calls for a quote for a product or service, I'll get the "new client quote checklist". The new client quote checklist lists all the questions and answers the new potential client may ask.

The follow-on process is "what do I do now" process, and again with a checklist. If the new client called and asked a question that isn't on your checklist, have a process on how to add and update the checklist. This may seem like overkill, because obviously you know how to answer the phone. What if you get so good at your job, you want to hire more people? How long is it going to take to teach them everything you know, and how many client calls are you going to miss while teaching them? What if you invested two weeks training them—then they quit. That would be two weeks of lost revenue and nothing to show for it.

When you own your own business, the goal is almost always to make money, then make MORE money. The bigger you get, the more checklists and processes you will need. Your goal may be to keep working and getting bigger until you die. Do you have a checklist of what should happen after you die – it's called a will? The number of processes and checklists can be endless. As you create new processes and checklists, you may want to print and put them in a binder to start your SOP.

Your SOP should be uniform, consistent and easy to understand by anyone, not just an employee or you. Consistent and uniform means they all

look the same and use the same terminology, objects or mapping keys. If you have an action step and you use a green arrow for one process and checklist, the same green arrow should be used for the other processes and checklist. One of the most common processes keys are themed around traffic signs and color. "If this, stop, yield or go [red, yellow, green] to this question or step. Why print it? What's your process for taking a lead when your computer crashes and everything is lost?

Checklist and Process Best Practices

The best checklists often have diagrams and screen shots for every single step, and literally say "double click left mouse button here" with a picture of the curser over the button. Some may even have a picture of a hand on a mouse with a big red arrow pointing at the mouse button. The idea behind a process or checklist is to give it to someone of no knowledge of the job or task and they should be able to complete the task without assistance. Using consistent icons or small pictures is better for flow and action steps. Simplicity is key.

- **EXAMPLE:** If you or a new employee is talking to a new lead on the phone your checklist should be simple bullet points with questions and potential answers. If it takes 30 minutes to read the checklist, the lead isn't going to wait, and everything will sound awkward and rehearsed.
    - o **TIP:** Once you have a process or checklist written down create a small script and have a friend of family member call you as a client (or you call them). Run through your checklist only, and only respond with what's on the checklist and get feedback. If it seems awkward, steps are missing or questions came up not on the checklist, <u>update it.</u>

When you first create a checklist and template use text boxes that will

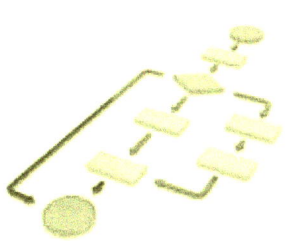 explain why each step matters or how they relate to a later step. When it comes time to add or remove steps you will remember why it was there in the first place. The explanation will help identify possible automation opportunities down the road. You SOP should have the actual checklist AND the explainer with text boxes.

Yes, this seems like a lot of work when all you want to do is start selling. However, if you don't do it before you start selling, when will you—after your process fails?

Processes in Perspective

"PRESS 1 if you are an existing customer". Larger companies automate as many systems as they can because it saves them money. Those systems aren't always the most efficient, and you may be on hold saying "representative" for an hour. Since one of your competitive advantages  "personalized service" maybe your first process is answering a call or calling a web lead. If the web lead doesn't want to speak, then the personal service likely isn't as important to them. You may find leads who don't want to speak aren't worth your time.

Automation and production lines are industrial age principles, with those same concepts repackaged for the digital age. Many processes in the digital age can be automated, however the more automation the less personal your service may be. Additionally, automation systems and software typically are monthly fee-based services, where the initial cost may not outweigh the benefit. In the long term, automation is the key to cutting expenses and freeing up time. If you've been to a grocery store, big box retailer, and many fast food and restaurants you've likely seen or used self-check-out systems, tablets or self-serve systems. Self-serve and check out systems eliminate the human error, but also the personal experience. A self-serve system or process works when you aren't, doesn't require hourly wages or health benefits and is never late.

Processes frequently automated:

- Customer Relationship Management (CRM)
- Lead Generation
- Customer Contact
- Invoicing and payment reconciliation
- Ordering, returns, refunds
- Supply Chain
- Digital Marketing
- Reviews and Referrals

A main street business or working from home may want to automate some or all of these processes. However, start the old-fashioned way and write down your key processes if you want to save money in the short term. Dozens of software platforms can accomplish these tasks, but they may provide more than you need, or miss the key and most important tasks for your business. Purchasing or signing a multi-year contract to automate one or two tasks that may be accomplished with ten minutes of manual labor daily may not be worth hundreds of dollars a month, especially if you are seasonal or only operate ten hours a week.

One of the most common automation solutions for a service-based business is a customer relationship management (CRM) system. A CRM system is a set of processes build into a software system to manage relationships or the status of clients through the business sales cycle. Many companies use them to track clients, and ensure their processes are being  accomplished efficiently. You can purchase or subscribe to a CRM system to run your business, but you will still want to make a checklist on how to use it. Most CRM systems automate or allow you to create rules within them on what to do next. Think of the last time you emailed a business and got a "Thanks for your message" response, or worse "The email box is not monitored- DoNotREPLY". Many CRM systems automate processes you may have, to include auto sending a "please leave a review" link. Often there are add on features for mass emailing, marketing and payment reminders or linking to an invoicing system for direct pay. Again, if your goal is to build a relationship with a customer and offer personal service, you may want to "personally" contact them in lieu of mass email and general templates. If a process is complicated, remember your hoagie and break it down to small pieces with a checklist for each piece. The key is the easier the better.

Do you need a CRM?

A CRM system may or may not be necessary for you and your business initially. It comes down to your budget, but more importantly what you are providing—a product or service. If you are selling tangible relatively inexpensive products, you may not need a full-fledged CRM system to track one-time purchases (OTP) or every person who bought a bottle of shampoo. This would be in an E-commerce sales report anyway. If you are providing a product that may require service after the sale, delivery, or installation a CRM system may be beneficial.

If you made the old-fashioned checklists, they are a starting point for selecting a CRM. Assessing your processes will help you determine if you need something fully customizable, or commercial of the shelf (COTS) system. Since a CRM system is an ongoing or continuous fee you will likely have a sales rep to work with. You can always send them your most important checklists or use the hard copies as a baseline for questions. "Does your CRM software do this" and get a demo.

- PROCESSES are if, then, what steps to take in your daily business activities
- CHECKLISTS are simple step by step guides on how to do every job-related task or function
- SOP is you combined manual of processes and checklists or employee handbook
- CRM is a software system used to track clients in multiple phases of the buying process

  Typical checklists nearly every business needs:
  - Inbound leads: phone, web, in person
  - Outbound communication: phone and web/email
  - Payment processing, payment refunds
  - Sending an invoice, cancelling an invoice
  - Hiring and firing an employee or independent contractor
  - Payment disputes, credits, or nonsufficient funds
  - Asking for referrals and reviews, responding to referrals and reviews
  - Ordering office supplies, fixing a jammed printer or replacing ink.

Creating process guides and checklists will decrease wasted time and increase the value of yours.

Chapter 4: BAM

When you met your significant other at that piano bar, you reminisce about that night. There certainly were other suiters, but the guy in the fedora ended up just being that—a hat aficionado. You still laugh about the group of girls wearing bathing suits since it was the middle of winter. There was the guy with his laptop complaining about the noise because he was working

on his screenplay, but who goes to a piano bar looking for quiet setting to write? Though ridiculous and probably inappropriate for the setting, those people still stood out to you.

Most budding entrepreneurs and business owners (new or old) confuse the purpose and differences between branding, advertising and marketing (BAM). If you did a quick search online for the differences, you'll find a hundred million results. There are dozens of opinions on the differences, and what a "push" or "pull" strategy is, as well as sub and sub-subsets.

To make things easier to understand; *branding is who you are on the inside, marketing is how you dress, advertising it telling people why they should like you.* You can change outfits, dye your hair and talk with a Boston accent but none of that changes who you are. If you just up and told everyone you know right now that you're from Boston and started talking with an accent some people may be curious, but many may just think you're trying to be something you're not.

As a small business owner, you don't need a Master of Business Administration (MBA) to have a successful marketing, branding, and advertising strategy, unless of course that's what your business is. It all starts with your ideal customer.

Ideal Customer - Persona

Who is most likely to buy, use and benefit from your product or service?

Do you want to hunt or fish for them? You can create an ad or promotion put it on a hook and toss it in the water and just wait. You may get nibbles here and there and every once in a while, you'll get a bite and reel it in. Inspecting your catch, it may have to be thrown back and your hook rebaited. Maybe it's a keeper, and it goes in the basket – but it may not be what you were fishing for, yet, you don't want to go home hungry.

You can go hunting instead, looking for something you specifically want, and your effort will determine the frequency in which you eat. You can hunt with a shotgun, which is good to cover a lot of area at short ranges, or a sniper rifle effective at most distances and you can see what you're hitting. **[PITFALL]** Many new businesses start with and adapt the mindset of I'll take any lead or business I can get. What if you did that with your significant other? You go home with the first person who talked to you at the night club, moved in together, and are engaged to be married? Sure, it may work out or you may have committed the rest of your life to living with a lazy, drunk, slob, who contributes nothing to the relationship and only brings your down in the long run.

Your Service Area

Are you hunting 'near me', nationally or internationally as previously discussed in your business plan? Are you fishing in a lake, or the ocean? Hunting in your back yard, or the Serengeti? If you're looking for a whale in a lake, or a Bison in your back yard, you may be there for a while. Who is your primary customer, or focus—B2B or B2C? Your ideal customer is the central focus to your business plan for branding, advertising and marketing. There are dozens of segmenting formulas; the four most common are demographic, psychographic, behavioral, and geographic. To put things in perspective, think about walking into a movie theater. You look up and see dozens of movies from horror, kids, romance, comedy, action, drama and sci-fi. Sure, you can go and see whichever movie you want, but which <u>will</u> you see and what brought you to the theater in the first place?

You may have multiple ideal customers and personas based off different products or services but start with the main reason you went into business and your core products.

Who will benefit from **<u>most or all</u>** your products and services? Many new entrepreneurs try to sell everything to everyone immediately and don't take the time to map out 'who' is most likely to buy. Unless you have an infinite marketing and advertising budget, starting with a sniper rifle will garner the best results until you have significant social proof.

PRODUCTS		SERVICES	
1 _____	2 _____	1 _____	2 _____

Looking at your core products or services, most main street businesses start with geographic and demographic segments. Behavior analysis and psychographic are important if you're looking nationally and internationally and have a large budget for focus groups and test markets. Start with yourself and your demographic. This is everything from your age, sex, race, relationship status, income, where you live, rent or own, your job, education, hobbies, and hangouts. You may not be targeting or trying to sell to people like you, but people tend to associate with people like themselves, and trust people <u>more</u> when they have things in common. If your ideal customer is nothing like you mapping out who you are will help with objection handling if and when the time comes.

The main criteria for targeted demographics, and a simple contrast of why they may matter are:

- **Age:** Would you trust a 19-year-old life coach?
- **Sex:** If you're having a baby who are you more likely to take motherhood advice from: a man, woman, or mother of three?

- **Race:** If your business is ethnic hair care products marketing to a bald white guy may be a waste of time?
- **Relationship status:** would you seek marriage counseling from someone who has never been married or been in a long-term relationship?
- **Income:** If you're a millionaire, would you take financial advice from someone who earns minimum wage?
- **Where you live:** If you're a farmer, would you trust a city slicker on how to live off the land?
- **Your job:** If you're a plumber, would you trust a writer to fix your toilet?
- **Education:** If you are selling or providing tutoring services for basic algebra, marketing it to college grads may be a waste of time.
- **Hobbies:** If you're a golfer, would you buy clubs from someone who's never golfed, or knows what the green is?
- **Hangouts:** Would you ask your grand mom what's the best nightclub for 20 something's?

All of these questions don't necessarily mean you wouldn't or couldn't, but it comes down to credibility and trust. If you are not like your ideal customer, you will have hurdles and objection handling down the road…if you get them in your door. No single factor will be the thumbs up, it's multiple factors.

- **EXAMPLE:** If you were in the market for a financial advisor, you may want someone younger than you since they will be working well past your retirement.

If your primary focus is business clients (B2B) it is similar to B2C with a few slight variations. Both have an age, an income level and a location to some extent. The big difference is the decision maker. With B2C the decision maker is likely the person you are talking to, or their significant other / family member. Within a business, it may be the owner, Chief Executive Officer (CEO), Chief Financial Officer (CFO), Chief Operations Officer (COO), Human Resources (HR) or anywhere in between. If depends on your product or service, and who decides to buy or not. If you walked into a coffee shop and told the first Barista you saw that you can sell them new/better cups for less, you're probably wasting your time. Similarly, if would be like trying to sell a new car to a 14-year-old. Chances are, they aren't writing the check...not always, but most of the time.

How old or what age range would most likely buy your product or service? Are they male or female? If you're selling or styling ethnic hair, your ideal customer likely is a specific race. Which ones? If you're a wedding planner, your ideal customer likely is single or recently engaged. If your product or service costs thousands of dollars, does your client have the money to even buy it? A 20 something may want a Ferrari, but that doesn't mean they can afford it. A surgeon who works 80 hours a week probably isn't in the market for a jackhammer. If you're a golf coach and instructor,

 you'll probably find more customers at a country club than an arcade. What type of services or products has your customer purchased in the past? Which social media platforms does your ideal customer use...most of the time? Where do they hang out, or go to regularly? If you're having trouble, start backwards. Who won't want, can't afford or won't benefit from your product or service? There are many other factors to consider including children, the presence of them in the home, their age range etc. These are the main categories, and they all have sub and sub-subcategories.

Once you identify your ideal customer, design your business and brand around them, not the other way around. A business that doesn't solve a problem or provide value won't be a business for long.

Your Logo

Your brand is who you are as a company, and it starts with your logo. A logo is a small image, word or icon that helps people find you in a crowd. Some businesses simply use their company name for their logo, others use a symbol or picture. Either way, it should relate to who you are, what you do, or what you stand for. It shouldn't be complicated, involve too much detail, or be so clever that it needs an entire story and explanation to understand. It can be a key product or service you provide or a combination of both.

QUICK TEST: If you put your logo on a piece of paper with multiple logo's that aren't household brands or names and showed it to someone what are the chances, they can figure out what you do, or who you are? A logo alone doesn't need to tell a whole story, but if it tells part of one you are moving in the right direction. If you add your one word from Chapter 2 next to your logo maybe a company name, what are the chances people will know what you do? If that piece of paper had all of the logos and all of the one-words could a stranger figure out what you do, then? Obviously, the paper is more crowded now and there's more information to sort through.

If you put your logo on a picture with no words or text can a stranger figure out what you do, sell or provide? An effective logo is identifiable with the minimum amount of information. If you printed that piece of paper in black and white, how recognizable are you then? **[PITFALL]** Creating or designing a logo that needs an entire story. Too much detail or color schemes.

- **EXAMPLE:** Think of every social media icon, electronic device in your house. Would you recognize it if it was only black and white?
  - o **TIP:** If you put your logo on a coin, and dropped it on the ground can you see and understand the logo?

One of the biggest mistakes people make with their logo is its complicated, multiple colors and has tons of detail. Sometimes they are very long, or multiple words or images and designs that have nothing to do with who they are—they just look cool. The best logo's and most recognizable are simple and convey a blatant or subconscious message without saying a word.

This book is sold on Amazon and hosted through Tiny Topic Books, so we will use them for our examples in branding, marketing and advertising. The logo shown on the side is simple, two T's in a book. At a distance, and in black and white it will still look like a book. Since  the T's are different colors, it draws your eye to recognize a letter or letters

Take a look at a few things in your house, your cell phone, your tv, the places you shop, the food or beverages you drink etc. If you needed to tell people what brands you have in your house or where you do most of your shopping, can you do it by describing the logo but not say the company name? If not, would they know if you JUST showed them the logo?

Your brand isn't likely a household name yet, but it may be at some point. When you think about the biggest brands, their logos can all be printed in black and white and still be very easy to see and understand. If the logo has words, it's usually minimal syllables. Millions and millions of dollars have been spent for you to know and understand those logos. Logos can turn in to status symbols, a T-shirt with no logo may cost $5. A T-shirt with some logos can cost hundreds and they are both made of cotton—not gold.

Look at the favicons in your web bookmarks (the little image in your web browser before a website URL or link). Seeing just the favicon, would your logo look clear right there?

One Picture, One Thing

Pictures speak louder than words. What one picture could tell someone about you and your company? It doesn't need to be complicated or dozens of pictures with all the things you do, just the main thing you do or provide? If someone saw this picture would they think of you, first? Many businesses provide a variety of products and services, but there typically is one or two central products or services they built on. Think of it as a specialization but general enough that a customer would know or assume you do other things. Once people trust you can do that one thing perfectly, they will feel more comfortable with the other things you do.

If you have that one picture, and you slapped your logo on it would they match or make sense? Would it convey clearly and concisely what you do or provide? Your one picture should be front and center on your webpage, social platform and business profile discussed later in this book.

- **EXAMPLE:** If you're a home-based travel agent, you could use a picture of an airplane. However, what if you don't want to sell plane tickets? Then that picture may not be the best option. If you focus on cruises, a cruise ship may be good – but what if cruises were only a small segment of your business and you focus on the experiences, not the boat?

What one picture would your ideal client relate to most? Who are they, and who are you? Is there a picture that would connect you to them, or a product/service that would provide value?

- **EXAMPLE:** If you're a carpenter, do you build houses, furniture, shelves, decks, gazebo's or something else? If you build decks, who for? Houses, or outdoor dining for restaurants? Fine tuning who your ideal customer is will simplify your message. Maybe your logo is simply a hammer with your initials.

Tag Line / Slogan

Can I buy you a drink? Once people see your one picture, your logo, and make the connection you are on your way. The next element is a statement or slogan. Successful brand statements and slogans convey your message about you, your brand, or a simple call to action to the potential client or customer. Most brand statements are 3-5 words, or if longer they don't have too many syllables. "15 minutes, 15%." Pragmatic juxtaposition of corporate identities wouldn't be a good slogan. The slogan can be about you, or your customer as long as it's easy to say and remember. Ultimately, if you can make it about you, your customer, or what you do and provide in less than five words you have a better chance of people remembering, saying, and associating it with you. Tag lines and Slogans are not the same thing. A tag line **IS** a slogan for specific products or services. When you first start marketing a brand-new business, you'll have a slogan. As you grow and begin to sell multiple products or services, each may have a tagline. Initially, they may be one in the same. A slogan or tag line is not your "mission statement", but your mission statement can have your tag line in it.

Tag lines can change over time, slogans less frequently, if ever. If you're unsure, test your slogan with a KPI for a year.

Tiny Topics
BIG IMPACT

- **EXERCISE:** Just do it.

Take a second and imagine a bunch of giant Clydesdale horses walking in a parade, what brand comes to mind? What if I said they were all dressed in red and white? Have a product yet? Now think of a separate but slightly related product that has the tag line: "_____, Australian for beer". What do the Clydesdales now represent of make you think of?

Putting a logo, your one picture, and tag line into perspective consider this. When you read: "**EXERCISE:** Just do it", did you think of a company or logo? Depending on your age, what would come to mind if I said: "Because you're worth it?"

You can change internally, but you'll likely still look like you. You can change your outfit every day, but you'll still have favorites. You can say something different to everyone you meet... but your logo, one picture and slogan do the talking when you aren't around.

Marketing

So, your brand is you. Marketing is what you wear, and more important what you were when you go to the "market". You grocery shop every Saturday at the same time in the same store, people with the routine may eventually recognize you. If you wore a uniform, or the exact same outfit every time people will recognize you quicker. As time goes on, you will become a pseudo comforting face or image to everyone who works there, and your fellow shoppers. You may never talk to anyone, but if you see a familiar person you may smile or acknowledge them before you would a stranger. You may even get mad if 'someone new' is in the cereal aisle screaming on their cell phone. But if that screaming customer is familiar you saw them last Saturday help an old lady get something from the top shelf, you may cut them some slack. Remember the bikini girls from the piano bar, it was just bikinis you remember not the people wearing them. You're more likely to notice and remember Fedora guy in the cereal aisle since he always wears a hat.

The more consistent you are within your market the more comfortable people will be with you. When you wear your favorite outfit you feel happy, proud and confident.   People see, feel, relate and potentially compliment you.   If you were wearing a skirt, a tuxedo blazer, combat boots and a space helmet you may get looks and attention, but no-one knows what you do.

Advertising

So, brand if is who you are, and marketing is what you wear consistently, advertising is what you say and do to attract people to you. Advertising can be broken down into hundreds of categories, but the primary reasons are three-fold: 1. Tell people who you are and build recognition 2. Remind people why they like you or provide social proof 3. Invite someone new to your brand, or sell something specific

When you think of advertising, most people think of 'sale'. Having a sale is a way to invite new people to your brand who may have heard of you, but don't know or trust you yet. If you have a dollar sign or a % on something you're advertising to sell something specific or invite someone new. **[PITFALL]** Brands that focus on price, pigeonhole themselves to always being about price. Unless you can mass produce your product or service, advertising with price will diminish or subconsciously suggest poor quality or service.

- **EXAMPLE:** Wholefoods doesn't advertise price, they advertise quality.

Have you ever seen a billboard for a beer or soda? Did it have a price, percentage or dollar sign on it? Was it a well-known brand? When you have brand recognition your advertising doesn't focus on price as much, if at all. Well-known brands advertise to remind people of their product, often not the price.

- **EXAMPLE:** Think of a commercial that has animated polar bears in red and white, what beverage are they drinking? You may see another commercial not long after with the slogan "same great taste, without the calories". The next commercial break may say, "12 pack of X $3.99 at your local grocery store this weekend!" Many new business owners are unclear when they take out an ad, buy a billboard, order postcard mailers or boost on social media to get new customers and clients. Before you spend a penny on advertising, what is the goal of your ad?

Hopefully you have a general understanding of your ideal customer, brands, advertising, and marketing. Strategies and specifics are covered more in depth in Chapter 8. If need be, go back and update your business plan as necessary. It's time to take a look at your digital face AKA your website.

PERSONA OR IDEAL CLIENT—the specific individuals or organizations that has a want, need and means to purchase your product or service

- TARGET MARKET is who you want to talk to, and want to trust your brand
- BRAND is who you are as a business
    o Logo, Slogan, One Picture
- MARKETING is what you wear, style dress and colors of your brand
- ADVERTISING is what you say to people to attract them to your brand
- SIMPLICITY IS KEY: this is who I am, how I look, and why we should talk.

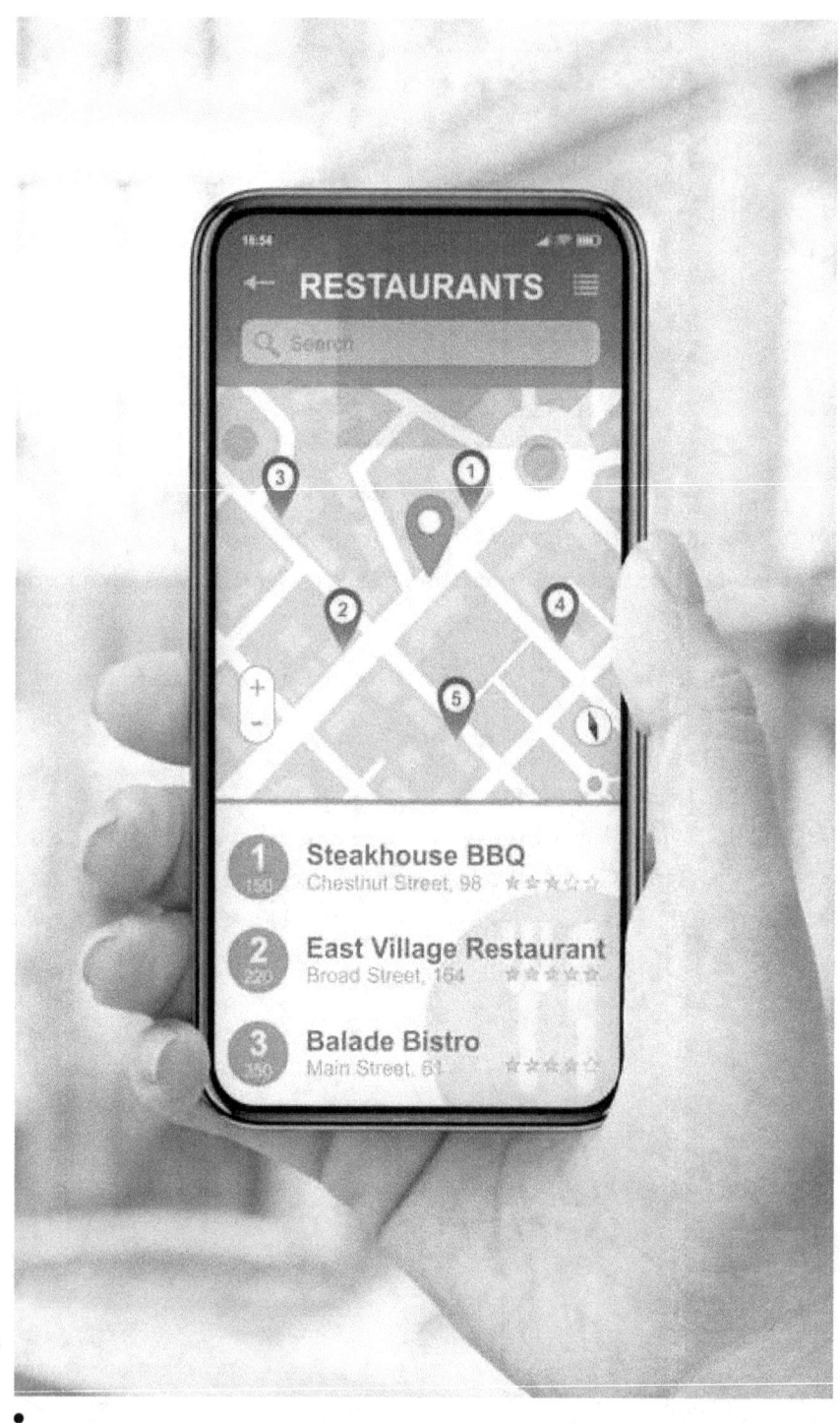

Chapter 5: First Impressions

So how did you meet your fiancé? Did you make eye contact with a warm smile (logo), walk up and introduce yourself (slogan) or send a drink across the bar (advertising)? First impressions are formed in about seven seconds when you meet someone new. There are eight components of a first impression. Handshake, tone and word selection, facial expression, energy, level of stress or relaxation, posture, dress and grooming, and eye contact. When you search online for something, be it a product, service or information it's like a blind date. Your website is who you are as a business, and the information above the fold is your digital face.

Maybe you're old fashioned and simply walked up to introduce yourself. Did you pitstop along the way and chat someone else up? When you went to speak, what if you had a huge piece of spinach in your teeth, and your breathe reeked of garlic? Your website is often your first, or in some cases your only chance to make a good impression and gain trust. Think about the last time you were looking for  information or a product online—or do a search now. When you type in, click a link did the page open immediately, or did it take a few seconds to load? Were you greeted with information, text or images directly related to what you searched for? Did the words and images or video match your search terms, and how did the landing page look? Was it busy, messy, incorrect spelling, poorly formatted, or outdated? Were there clear signals and signs to buy, contact, or request more information? If you request information or call, is it easy or does it involve multiple steps? Were you invited to stay, or actively engaged? MOST importantly, could you read the entire landing page in seven seconds or less? If not, were you guided to a next step? How long did you stay before you hit [BACK]?

If you've ever been on a blind date, or met someone face to face after first meeting online, how did it go? Were they as good or better than expected most of the time? If they looked nothing like their picture, had poor grammar, dressed like a slob you may have felt misled or ultimately were disappointed. If someone sets you up on the blind date you may cut them slack or be on the lookout for the good you heard and ignore the bad.

The point is your business starts with your website, regardless if you operate a storefront, work from home, or otherwise. If your website is a mess, it doesn't matter how great your product or service is, because no-one new will take the time to find out. Your storefront can be immaculate, but if your website looks like crap – 'new' clients will assume the same.

Of the millions of websites, they all have specific functions and purposes yet there's consistency within the categories. Your home or landing page is where it all begins, this is your first impression, or your digital face. An old newspaper phrase is "above the fold" meaning the information on the front page, at the top above where the paper gets folded. Since over 70% of web searches are done on mobile sites, you have a very limited amount of space. If people like your face, they may check out your outfit by scrolling down, or listen to what you have to say (click through). If they don't see, hear, have a chance to ask questions—or they smell something fishy, they will hit [BACK]. If they like what you show them, address their search terms, let them speak to you and you don't look like click bait, the will [BUY NOW] or [REQUEST INFO].

Types of Websites

Before going into depth of what should be above the fold and why, first determine the differences in site categories. If you're not sure how you site should look, check out your competition with the best ratings. Most websites fit within one of the following categories, and many have overlap to some extent.

- Entertainment
- Information and research
- Advertising
- E-commerce
- Services
- Social proof

If you do a quick internet search for the top "most clicked websites" you'll see social media and more importantly "social proof" websites dominate in the top 20 and 50. Within the various types of sites, visitors spend different amounts of time. Entertainment and information or research sites by far have the most visitors per month who stay on the page for extended periods of time.

- **EXAMPLE:** Think social media, news, and video sharing sites.

Although nearly every site advertises, some specifically are designed to get clicks and reroute you to a product, service or other page. Think of click bait sites, job sites and many blogs. They offer you a little relevant information, but usually link to a sponsor or someone who paid them to get referrals and leads.

E-commerce sites are where you can buy something through an automated system or process with easy workflows. They typically have 'cart' functions, accept payments directly through the site, and require little to no human to human interaction. Some have chat windows and bots to help, or massive FAQ sections.

Service based sites typically are for more complicated purchases requiring some form of human interaction like consulting, or customized products and services.

Lastly are the social proof sites, these are the review, compliant and Q&A forums for anyone who used the other types of websites or businesses. These mainly focus on e-commerce, products and services and they often sell advertising space to businesses who sell products or services.

Knowing the purpose of each site, the key question is, "what are you trying to accomplish with your website?" More importantly, what do you want site visitors to do? This will determine what kind of site you should have, and how to convert them into customers.

What kind do you need?

The main types of sites for Main Street or Home-Based businesses are advertising, e-commerce or service. The other types of sites will certainly be important, and we will cover how and which ones to use and leverage to build your business. First let's run through a few scenarios and questions to clarify the differences so you can determine what site you should have. The assumption is you  would rather have customers hit [BUY NOW] instead of [BACK].

E-Commerce

If your business is to sell tangible products (something you can physically hold) you *may* need an e-commerce site. If you have or want an ecommerce site, you will want to make multiple process checklists. Before buying, designing and investing in an e-commerce site, these questions will help determine of you really need one:

1. Where is the product produced?
   EXAMPLE: A factory, sweatshop, or your living room, basement, garage etc.?

2. Is the product premade or customizable/made to order?
   EXAMPLE: A frozen pizza with everything, or you choose the toppings?

3. Does your product or service start with a base template or is it customer driven specifications?
   EXAMPLE: A T-shirt may be [S], [M], [L], [XL] a dress shirt can be made and cut to your body dimensions, chest, waist, neck, etc.

4. Can the customer do everything to customize without talking to you or a person?

You can have an e-commerce site for all the above scenarios, but that doesn't mean you should. E-commerce sites are time consuming, expensive to create and maintain and there are many associated additional fees with order processing, taxes, supply chain, shipping and waste/returns. When you first start out selling your wares, or to add an additional avenue/revenue stream consider e-commerce consolidators. E-commerce consolidators allow you to list and create a store on their website for minimal fees, that are point and click to add, change. list and modify your products. Most offer additional services for warehousing products, supply chain functions (packing, shipping, returns) and they provide simple sales  reconciliation and accounting functions. If you're starting small, look at the largest ecommerce sites in the top 50 'most clicked', and you may want to sell, ship or process through them at first. They have all the cart functions, payment processing, do some advertising similar to social media boosting. They do charge fees, and some have commissions, but the are far less in comparison to creating production line, maintaining storage space and managing a supply chain. The biggest e-commerce consolidators are Amazon, Walmart, and Etsy. E-bay is also used, but they aren't as comprehensive with supply chain and fulfillment.

If you go this route, you simply create an information site to collect customer data and provide more information and social proof. A separate buy tab would link directly to your consolidator's fulfillment page. Once you are selling products and generating a profit, you can easily determine if you can increase profit by starting your own e-commerce site or phase yourself away from the consolidator.

E-Commerce Fully Customizable with Template

If you don't want to use a consolidator, and/or your products are fully customizable by the customer without you or employee interaction, then you will need an e-commerce site. You will also need many processes and checklists to handle who and what to do once a product is submitted for order. Vistaprint.com, Art.com and Queensboro.com are examples. If there is minimal customization, like engraving or simply adding text or an image to a product, you may be able to still use a consolidator and just have special instructions or free text for all purchases. If you do not deviate from a standard template, you may benefit from an e-commerce site with clickable options and short free text fields.

- **EXAMPLE:** Pizza (clickable topping options), Jewelry (engraving free text) T-shirts or hats with text or logo within specific areas of the products. (image upload)

E-Commerce Built to Order / Non-Template

If you sell a <u>fully customizable product</u> requiring personal interaction or communication at some point you may be better off with a service-based site and an invoicing system for payments and processing. Meaning, you are providing a product built or made to a customer's specifications, not based off templates. If you require payments or deposits a separate CRM will track payments and steps within the process throughout completion. Typically, this is the best option for larger or high dollar purchases for products that are not mass produced or only a limited number are produced annually.

- **EXAMPLE:** A custom desk or furniture.

Service Based Websites:

Most main street businesses whether brick and mortar, or home based revolve around providing a service. These services run the gambit from labor, consulting, skilled trades, research expertise, planning, delivery, design or installation. Whether you're a babysitter, dog walker, painter, electrician, web designer or travel agent you will need a service-based site. If you have one already, the chances are your site tries to be too much and it's losing you customers. **[PITFALL]** Service based sites that present themselves as e-commerce or provide information that allow customers to DIY. Taking Search Engine Optimization (SEO) out of the equation for now, most service-based sites are too large, or try to function as a research and information hub and/or E-commerce. Simplify your site.

If your business is a service, knowledge work, or you offer to 'do the research' or 'help customers chose' don't eliminate yourself from the process. Many service-based sites provide so much information that the visitor can make informed decisions without the service provider. Basically—you taught a visitor that they don't really need to contact you. You gave them all the information, explained the product and processes, and now they will just price shop you. If you're goal is to gain a new client who will rely and trust you to do the work and research, don't add information on your site on how they can do it themselves. Unless your site has a [BUY NOW] button that will collect payment, there is no reason to teach someone how to do it themselves. There are information and research sites that do this, and they earn money by selling ad space.

Service Based Businesses

Again, what is the purpose of your site? If your site isn't e-commerce, you really don't need advertisements or pricing front and center IF the visitor can't buy it right then and there. You can set baselines with a 'starting at' or 'from' prices, but a [CONTACT] button should practically be on top of the price. Again, none of this should be above the fold especially if you are a reseller. What's a reseller? If you are purchasing or putting together a package for a client by choosing multiple products or services available direct elsewhere, you're a reseller.

- **EXAMPLE:** If your business wedding planning, and you say '5 tiffany vases for centerpieces, 10 crystal dishes, Joes DJ service for 4 hours' all for $999.00, what do you think the visitor will do next? If they can't buy it that second, one of two things will happen. 1. They call you if you have a call-to-action button or 2. They independently research the cost of the centerpieces, crystal dishes

and Joes DJ service. If they do call you, and you don't pick up –
they are calling Joes DJ next. **Client Lost**

If every time you add a price if it has an asterisk with fine print and
additional terms and conditions, people won't trust you. There are rules and
laws requiring terms and conditions if and when you add pricing. However,
your site basically is presenting as e-commerce, providing information to
DIY, and misleading (in the client's eyes) because people don't read fine print
when they are in the exploratory phase of purchasing. As soon as you tell
them that's the starting price, they feel it's a sales pitch and upsell, and you're
behind the power curve.

If you provide a service, they second you provide or add a price on your
website, you are triggering visitors to price shop you instead of value your
service. If you don't have a way to mass produce that service, you will always
be higher than a competitor who can.

Web Design

Before you design your website and take the below advice, look at the
products and services you own and use. What is your service or business,
and research the top providers
of that service or product and
check out their website? Do
lawyers, contractors, daycares,
travel agencies, plumbers,
graphic designers have pricing
on their website? Legal sites
may have pricing for DIY
services (incorporation), but

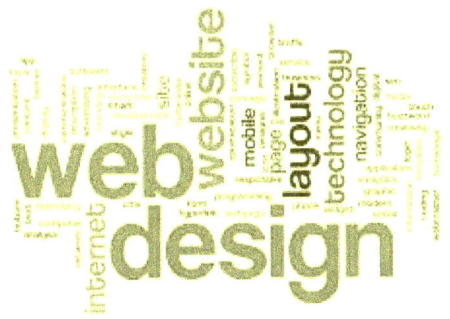

you aren't likely to see an actual lawyers' hourly rate. Plumbers may have
pricing to unclog a drain, but not likely install a new underground sewer line.
You can buy a cruise through and cruise website or the thousands of e-
commerce travel sites, but if a client can't immediately 'BUY NOW' through
your site you are devaluing your service.

If you already have a website and its service based, how does it look? Do
you check the visitor statistics, and click through rates? If your existing site
generates dozens of qualified leads, buyers, and clients **per day** – don't fix
something that isn't broke. If you simply want more, improve the SEO and
develop a new digital marketing stream. If you have limited visitors, rarely
get a new lead, call, or qualified enquiry this information will be invaluable.

If you have a service-based business, you probably want [CONTACTS] not [CLICKS]. Ten qualified contact us now is better than 10k clicks per month if no-one contacts you. If you want contact, what's above the fold is more important than anything else on your site. If you are just remarketing products or services sold elsewhere with an exclusive deal*** you're not a service site, you're an advertising site. If you aren't paid per click, don't get [CALL NOW] leads, your site is a waste of time and money. To redesign your site above the fold, this is what you need:

1. **Your company name, logo, slogan, 1 picture or video.**
   - Your one picture, or a short looping video (10-30 seconds) – not a slider. Sliders are for e-commerce sites to display multiple [BUY NOW] options. Many sites use sliders, but they are either too slow or too fast, especially if they have text more than 5 words. Sliders slow sites down, and if it's the first thing someone sees, is it answering a question the visitor has? Does the next slide, or the one after? Again, you have seven seconds to tell the visitor who you are, what you do, and why use you. If you really want a slider, put it below the fold.

2. **50 words or less.**
   - Say what!? Yes, 50 words or less, including your name, the tab names, the words 'call now', your slogan included. If you have more than three sentences visible on your landing page, a visitor

may read one. If that one doesn't convince them to read more, they are gone. Remember, 70% of web searches and services are found on a mobile device. If you look like the right suite, they will scroll below the fold.

3. **Three EASY ways to contact you immediately as buttons.**

- [CALL NOW] [REQUEST QUOTE] [MORE INFO]. Each button should do something and start a process for you. Call now starts your answering the phone process and check list [high priority client]. Request quote starts the sending a quote process and checklist [medium priority client]. More info starts the more info process and checklist [low priority client].
    - Fourth button: collect data and subscribe.

Tip: Regardless of how they contact you, you may want to call them right away. The easiest way to build rapport is calling. If you just make a quote and send it if it's undeliverable or the wrong number—the quote time is wasted. You are a personal service, prove it and be a person. "I got your request; I'll get back with a quote shortly." Calling right away is the fastest way to save time and assess whether you are working with your ideal client or a time waster. If they don't want to talk (ever) then service may not be important.

[CALL NOW] should link and call you or whoever answers your phone immediately. Since most people search the web via their phones or devices it should auto-call. A big bright button, not your phone number. You can have your phone number listed, but it's better to have it on your contact page, header or footer. Put yourself in their shoes. If you were on the go, found a service but it only had the phone number as text instead of a button – do you have a pen? A phone number adds unnecessary steps.

[REQUEST QUOTE] This should link to or open a free text field with mandatory information. It can link to your contact page or an anchor on your home page, however a small pop-up with name, phone, email and free text field works best. This will allow their device to collect and add more cookies in their device, and they can keep searching and reading after they submit.

[MORE INFO] This should link to your contact page or anchor that has more info about your business, a contact form and a subscriber collector [Subscribe for more info/deal/news/etc.]

The fourth button above the fold. If your header freezes, meaning it's visible regardless of scrolling or what page you are on, add another button that is <u>YOUR</u> preferred contact method [CALL NOW] [REQUEST QUOTE] [MORE INFO]. When someone scrolls down passed your initial call to action buttons, if they find what they are looking for your preferred contact method is still there, and they don't have to go back and look for it. If you site meets or exceeds the visitor's initial expectations, meaning they stayed longer than 7 seconds do not make they have to click around or find your contact button.

Check out a few other service-based websites or think about the last one you used. How long were you on that site, and did it have enough info to DIY?

What was your one word in the business plan? Search it with 'near me' and again take a look at how their sites are set up and you may see themes with the ones that are top rated or have the biggest share of the market.

Below the Fold [Content]

If you're a service-based business, you don't need dozens of pages or tabs at the top of your website. Multiple tabs and subtabs are for research websites, e-commerce, or advertising sites. Most service-based businesses can be one long anchored page or have minimal tabs for image galleries, before and after, or videos. Images and videos on you home page will slow it down.

You will need content at some point for search engines to find you, but that doesn't necessarily mean that content must be visible on your site. This will be covered in the SEO section, but let's first talk about below the fold.

Social proof, awards or recognition from other trusted sites, vendors, or customers belong immediately below the fold. Anyone who isn't sure if you're the right site will feel more comfortable if they see social proof. Key products and services simplified (a short sentence or paragraph—anything longer than 3 sentences show have a 'read more' expansion or have hover

over text, each with a call to action button.

'About Us' section. Many businesses think 'About us' should be the first thing visitors should see, that is simply wrong. It should be 'About you-the customer' meaning about the problem you will solve for the visitor.

- **EXAMPLE:** What cell phone do you have? Go to their website, is the first thing their life story or what they have to offer to you?

Your 'About us' section will be the bulk of your text and have the majority of your SEO content and words. This is where you should match the key search terms, words and metadata. If the search terms were 'corporate lawyer near me' this section should say "I'm a corporate lawyer near you."

Often new businesses, and even more often older business have too much information on their landing page, or simply too much information overall on their website. Most of it doesn't need to be front and center or can be removed completely. If your page looks like click bait, or if the potential customer must click more than twice to find what they are looking for, the third click is [BACK] to the search engine.

- **EXAMPLE:** When you meet someone new do you want to hear their life story and how many cats they have? Maybe... if you're looking for an animal shelter or how to adopt, otherwise it's not likely.

Treat your website home or landing page like a first date! Who are you, what do you do, and how can we get or stay in contact? Look at some of the products you own, or services you use – what does their landing pages look like? Even if you love your website, if people don't contact you through it then it's a waste of time and money. You change, adapt or die.

One of the most important elements for new business outside their websites is social proof and search engine optimization—so let's delve into that now.

- Your website is your first impression and your digital face
- You have seven seconds to make an impression and keep someone on your website
- Websites primarily fall in to one of the following categories:
    o Entertainment
    o Information and research
    o Advertising
    o E-commerce
    o Services
    o Social Proof
- Most small and home-based businesses are service based, with few requiring e-commerce
- Service-central business landing pages should be simple with a minimum three calls to action
- Company name, logo, slogan, and calls to action should be prominent and easy to read
- Above the fold landing page should be simple with 50 total words or less.
- Your website should generate leads, **not teach people** how to DIY.

Chapter 6: Social Proof

Where and how did you actually find and meet your fiancé? Maybe it <u>was</u> the piano bar, maybe the grocery store or you sat next to them for years in class or the office. Did you find them, or did they find you? Were you set up through a friend or family member? The small business environment has changed tremendously in the last twelve months. Some industries are closing faster than opening, and those still around have limited staff and hours or skeleton crews.

Social proof is perhaps the most important aspect for a Main street or home-based business. It's one of the easiest and least expensive ways to generate new leads and customers yet many small businesses simply don't do it consistently. Social proof is like being set up by a friend or family member. They feel they know you well enough to suggest someone else you may like. Social proof is a customer's opinion of you as a business and it bares more weight than anything else you can do. Social proof is divided across four channels:

1. Business Profiles
2. Social media
3. Review Sites
4. Consolidator sites

Regardless of your business type, you will need all four to thrive post pandemic. All increase and contribute to Search Engine Optimization (SEO) and your websites visibility. One may be more important than the others depending on your business type, however creating, updating and monitoring all should be a regular and consistent process with mile stones and KPI's.

SEO and Near Me

"Near Me" - The two small words that can have the greatest impact on any service business. Business type plus "near me". Most searches for services happen on mobile devices, but they won't find you unless you have a service area or associated postal code.

If you want people to find you on the 'World Wide Web' you will need to have key terms and data that search engines can find and see. There are many components of search engine optimization including content, indexing, meta tags, scrolling and crawling, backlinks among just a few. This data can be found by search engines in text, video's or images. This book isn't designed to teach how to write code and DIY all your SEO. However, it will cover the things you can and should do, whether you have SEO or code writing experience or not.

First, SEO is not a one-time thing, it is a constant regular practice with required updates to target the most relevant search terms. If you want to

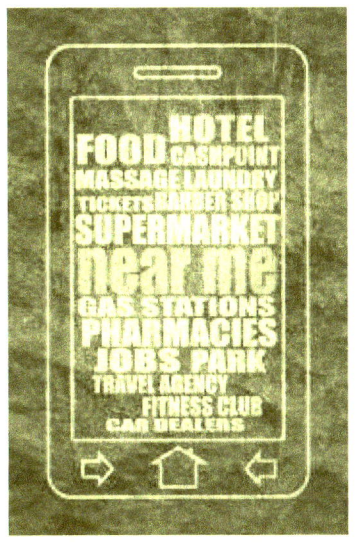

rank high on search engines consistently without paying ad premiums, SEO is the starting point. Your site can get to the top as sponsored businesses, but if your service area is worldwide it won't be easy or cheap. The larger the service area you have the more involving it gets because you are competing with other 'near me' options. SEO primarily looks at content plus words plus word strings and the quantity of each throughout the site. Think about the last time you were looking for information or a product online or do a search now. If you typed it in a simple search string, clicked a link and the page opened how long did you

look for your search on that page? If that page opened and didn't immediately show you what you were looking for, or there were thousands of words and images what did you do next? Did you read and sort through everything, or did you hit 'BACK' and check a different site?

If you've been following and think back to your 'digital face' aka your website, the suggestion for your landing page was simple and limited words. Seems counter-productive if you're trying to be found online and content plus words are a key factor, right? You can have all the words and content added to your site without necessarily making it cluttered or looking like click bait. You can create a paragraph, or multiple paragraphs with all the search terms and word string variations for your site. However, that doesn't mean a visitor has to see all this gobbled goop, you can add it with the tiniest font, and make it transparent or the same color as your site background. Search engines look for data, tags, and words – not whether a human can see it. You can embed multiple words, tags and data directly in images if you know what you're doing. The easier way is put them in your header or footer but preview your site before posting to make sure you can't see them.

If you work from home, you may not want to add your home address for people to find you. If that's the case and it usually is, make sure you define and specify your service area. If your goal is local marketing or in specific regions or post codes, make a list of the post codes to add in the paragraph.

- **EXAMPLE:** Auto detailer near me, auto detailer near 90210, car detailers near 90210, top auto detailers 90210 etc.

Masking Keywords

Below the fold you have "about" sections, service offerings and other business-related information, basically longer paragraphs. Let's say your website background is white, and you are using 14-point black font and you have three short paragraphs. Instead of just hitting 'return' or having space in between each paragraph, write search terms and tags at 7-point font in white. When a visitor sees the page, it will simply look like you have a paragraph space, but the relevant search terms and strings are simply hidden between the paragraphs.

#HASHTAGS

#HASHTAGS are word strings related to a topic, often used in social media. If your service has relevant hashtags, you may want to add them as well or just make some up. They are indexed easily, and whether someone is talking about you specifically or not, when people search, you may just pop up. Whenever you write content, add or post a picture, and reach out to new customers add a #HASHTAG relevant to you, or create a new one that identifies your business. You may not be a big social media user, and it may

not be a big component of your marketing but having them will make those who are find you easier.

Image Tagging/Labeling

If you've ever done a search for images only, the ones that pop up have been tagged or labeled with your search terms or are on a page with your search terms. Don't just call your picture what it is, use your business-related search terms as well. Don't say "Chicken Sandwich", say "Chicken Sandwich Joes Deli 90210"

SEO firms and professionals charge anywhere from $200 to tens of thousands a month, hour, or even per word string. I know what you may be thinking if you ever looked into hiring a SEO pro…$200 a month, year right!? More like $2000 a month! Maybe, but not really have you ever searched [SEO freelancer]?

- **TIP:** Start small until you get some traction if you don't want to invest a ton of money. A few zipcodes until you see results (have milestones and KPI's to check) then add more once you see it working and want to increase your service area.
  - **EXAMPLE:** Be the top result in your neighborhood, then town, then county then state and so on.

You can increase your SEO and website visibility without writing code, hiring a pro, or spending a boatload of money through business profiles, social media, reviews, and consolidator sites as well—but you need to be consistent and wear the same outfit throughout.

Business Profiles

"I'm listed in the phone book" has been replaced with "Google my Business". That doesn't mean the phone book doesn't exist anymore. The 'old fashioned' hardcopy phone book may be rarer, but the yellow pages still maintain a website with all the same information. Every business, large or small, main street or your street can register and claim their businesses through a variety of business profile sites. Business profiles have merged and  morphed with many social media platforms, or the social platform allows you to create a standalone profile for your business.

Business profile sites for the most part offer free basic packages to list your business which may be all you need. Many profile sites sell or offer 'premium' profiles for one time, or a monthly fee. They are different then consolidator or social media sites, but they operate the same way. Again, business profile sites have a lot of overlap with social media and consolidators.

The main sites you should create and maintain a profile:

- Google my Business
- Yellowpages.com
- Yelp
- Better Business Bureau (BBB)
- Pinterest
- Manta

By far the most used and trusted is Google my Business. I know it sounds crazy, because you'd think the yellow pages or BBB would be more trusted, and perhaps they are but when was the last time you checked reviews on those sites, or posted a GOOD one? Over 90% of people use Google as their preferred search engine, so  naturally it's in Googles best interest to feature their products and services first. If you 'Google' BBB reviews on a company name, you may see the Google reviews before the BBB site, or have multiple click to get there.

There certainly are more business profile sites than what we listed, and Pinterest borders the line from a business profile site and a product review site, hence overlap. Business profile site typically earn money through subscription or 'premier status' whether the business is good or not...with exception to Google. Google pages show up through the entire internet if you are using them as a search engine, where the premier services on the other profile site only top-rated businesses within their site. With that, you can be a big fish in a smaller pond via yelp, for the same price of a small fish in a big pond via Google sponsored ads. Basic profile for all of these sites are free, and with that every business should list with them. That doesn't mean your goal is to advertise or use them, but it supports SEO and indexing.

If you work from home, you may not keep regular hours or have a physical address you want listed. When people search "near me" whatever device they are using tracks their search, shopping history, and where they are. Unless they specifically clear caches of data on their device regularly, it is on there somewhere. Whether they use a map or GPS function, direction request from or to a certain place, or 'checked in' at a location. Maybe they sent a friend a picture of their lunch and said, "I'm at XYZ diner".

If your site, social pages, or business is ubiquitously registered in the 'world' it's less likely you will be associated 'near them'. The solution for a savvy owner will find and register a mailing address as your location, typically by getting a post office box. If your service area is mainly your town and/or surrounding towns the focal point address should be a post office, or other government entity with a physical location and post code. However, clearly note it as a mailing address, not services to be performed at address. If you want something that has an actual street address, ups stores offer post boxes with street addresses.

Established physical locations that tend to not change have been and are likely indexed already—like government buildings. The goal is to tell search engines: "I'm near that, if you're near that, you're near me". Post office boxes are typically $10-20 a month depending on your location, if you get one save the receipt for your proforma.

Social Media

Since entertainment sites are frequented more than all other sites combined, getting social with your brand and business has never been more important. Again, consistency is key—whatever you display on your website, and now your business profile listings should be consistent with what you show in your social media. Remember the grocery store, you don't have to talk to people for them to become familiar with you.

Not all social media is created equally, and though most people have some sort of social media presence it really is different strokes for different folks. The question comes down to marketing, and who is your ideal customer or client—meaning who do you want to sell to most of the time?

The top social media platforms for business, both e-commerce and service based are Facebook, Instagram, Twitter, LinkedIn, YouTube, Reddit, Pinterest, and Quora. Other platforms are getting more involved like messenger, Whatsapp, Tiktok and a few others. It almost seems like a full-time job just to be on or have a presence on each of these sites, but don't worry... There are many other apps and services that post and repost everywhere for you.

- **EXAMPLE:** Sproutsocial.com

Before investing half your life online creating, updating and modifying the dozens of social media sites, and business profiles think again about your ideal customer. Of course, whoever buys from you is an ideal customer, but you'll need to narrow your scope and really focus on your customer persona. Facebook is by far the largest when comparing users plus business tools and functionality, but if you are looking to market to teens it may not be the best option. Each platform has different types of users and demographics even though there is a lot of overlap.

Don't put all your eggs in one basket, but don't kill yourself to keep an egg in EVERY basket, choose one or two that will be your primary focus. If you are trying to sell to people just like you, which social platforms do you use the most and have you ever bought or trusted an ad enough to buy or click through to it? If your ideal client or customer is nothing like you, which platform do they use the most? To get you started, here is a simple breakdown of who used what the most in 2020.

- **Facebook:** Slightly more female than male, mostly 30 years or older, higher income and education levels.
- **Instagram:** More female than male, the bulk are 29 years and younger. The older you are, the less likely you use it. One third

of users earn less than $30k a year.

- **Twitter:** Far more male users than female, most users between 18 and 49. two thirds report some or college degrees.
- **LinkedIn:** Far more male users then female, 70%+ college educated nearly half users earn more the $75k a year
- **Pinterest:** Three to one female over male users all age groups with the bulk 30-49. 40% earn over $75k
- **Snapchat:** Even between male and female users. 70% are teens 13-17, and the bulk of all users are younger than 29. Lower reported income and college education.
- **YouTube:** More male than female, all age demographics largest user group is 25-30 years old. Higher reported income and the highest reported college educated users.

So, what does this mean, and more importantly what does it mean to you as a business owner? It comes down to what platforms are best to reach your IDEAL customer. Since Snapchat is primarily teens, advertising home healthcare for seniors probably isn't going to get many new customers. Facebook on the other hand may be a better option. Ultimately, you'll also want to know and determine who makes the buying decision for specific products or services.

Reviews

The old saying is if you have a bad customer service experience, you'll likely tell 10+ people, whereas a good one you'll only tell a handful. The reality is more people tend to leave reviews only when they have a bad experience. That doesn't mean they don't or won't leave a good one, but it may just be a little more work on your part.

People check reviews before making purchases, going somewhere new, or doing anything they haven't done before. In fact, there is an entire industry that revolves around it. If you look through the top visited websites clicked in a month, many of them are review and customer experience sites. It is perhaps the most important aspect to a business AND a potential consumer.

But…not all reviews or sites are created equally. Many businesses auto send review links to clients. They often are internal, and if the review is bad it likely won't be displayed anywhere. Naturally, businesses want to boost and protect their reputation, so many reviews are used for corrective actions instead of feedback for other customers. These businesses can pick and choose what reviews will be posted to the public, and of course you can 'buy' reviews through dozens of nefarious sites, legal and honest or not…it still happens. Many large businesses and social proof sites require you have an account in order to submit a review, or they annotate if the review is verified based off whether an actual purchase being made. Reviews and feedback can be collected and submitted almost everywhere, and often multiple sites for just one purchase. They all have ways and means to evaluate and validate reviews or give the owners the option to dispute.

Google My Business (GMB) and Google reviews are more trusted than other sites because there isn't a specific business relationship. Having 10,000 five-star reviews on a smaller or internal system with no bad feedback is fishy to most customers. Google reviews are more trusted because it's very difficult to submit a review without having an 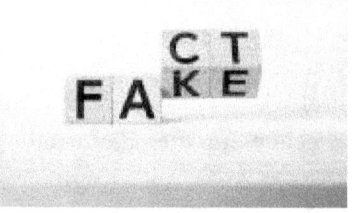 associated Gmail, or email address. You can submit Google reviews without Gmail, but it requires many more steps, and people often don't take the time. This may hurt businesses if they don't help or make the review process simple. It's a catch 22 because the only way to get google reviews is having, verifying and registering with GMB.

If you have a GMB profile, you will be auto indexed for search engines, and if you verify your business it happens quicker, and reviews can be posted sooner. Whatever information you added on your website should be consistent or as close as possible with all your business profile platforms. Where and when possible, use the same descriptions, images, videos and word strings so when people search you, you end up being all the results on the page but through multiple websites. Remember fedora guy, and bathing suit girls. If everything is the same across all platforms, you become more consistent and trustworthy.

Bad Reviews

Unfortunately, there is nothing preventing someone from creating fake reviews for businesses they never used or visited. Someone with hundreds of email addresses can tank a business before it gets off the ground. There is hope. If the review is legitimate, whether you agree or not, quickly and professionally respond and contact the customer if possible. A few nice words may change their mind or simply remove the review. Apologize and mention you will be reaching out shortly to remedy the issue. If it's a fake, unfair or simply non-constructive reach out to the company hosting the review and ask for it to be removed immediately. The emphasis is RESPOND, and respond professionally, and try to make things right. Calling a reviewer or customer an A-hole publicly can cause more damage than the bad review. If they and the review site refuse to change the review or take it down, just move on. Some companies with terrible reputations completely rebrand and start over.

- **TIP:** When responding to good reviews, add your #HASHTAG at the end, and if the review didn't mention you or your company by name, add it in somehow. This will increase views and visitors to your GOOD work or products.
    - o **EXAMPLE:** Thanks for reviewing us Joe, you were a pleasure to work with, and we are glad to have finished the job before your Birthday. We at Marks Tree Service pride ourselves on fast turn around and high-quality customer service. Thanks again, Mark. #MarksTreeService

Customer reviews and social proof will likely bring you more business in the first year, then just about any ad campaign. As a new business looking for customers you will have a choice to spend time or money. Your best investment for your first year will be chasing and persistently getting reviews. Any marketing strategy or ad may get someone to check you out, but without

social proof, they it likely ends right there. A marketing campaign or advertisement is one off, where a great review lasts forever. Create a process checklist with KPI's for reviews, and diligently work at it.

Consolidator Sites

Outside your website, business profiles, and social media many reviews are available and often more prominent on advertising and consolidators sites. Consolidator sites are generally a combination of review platform, advertising, and lead generators. Most consolidator sites are designed for specific categories or industries. One of the biggest for e-commerce is Amazon. Reviewing a product on Amazon's platform doesn't necessarily get repopulated elsewhere. You may be a bestseller on Amazon, but don't expect to be number one in the New York Times. Most consolidator sites will allow a business to create a basic profile for free.

Example Consolidator Sites:

Trip Advisor	Food, restaurant, travel
Angies List	Service Businesses
Foursquare	Any Business, mostly restaurants
Amazon	E-commerce
Zillow	Real Estate
Realtor.com	Real Estate
Wedding Wire	Bridal Services
Thumbtack	Service Businesses
Home Advisor	Real Estate, home improvement

Consolidator sites earn money through multiple revenue streams to include advertising, lead generation, premier listing services, to fees and commission per sale. Though you can sign up for free, if you want lead generation you will have to pay in most cases. Even when an individual selects your business or profile and requests information if you are a non-paying profile, the lead *may* go to other similar paid businesses as well. Often, with a free profile the customer would need to contact you directly and not through the site if they want to use your service.

- **EXAMPLE:** If you are a free profile for roofing and someone sees your listing and requests you call, that request may go to you but will ALSO go to multiple local roofers with paid subscriptions.

Additionally, some sites are not just the host, but a major contributor or stake holder of the listed products and services…Meaning they are more likely to recommend their products and services before yours, regardless if you paid or not.

- **EXAMPLE:** You sell office supplies on Amazon; you are competing with Amazon Basics. Who do you think will show up first for free?

If you want to optimize searchability without spending money, create business profiles on every available relevant site for your business. Measure and check each site monthly, and if you receive results or enquiries from specific one, it may be beneficial to upgrade to a premium profile. The most important social proof and review site for any home based or main street business is GMB.

- Search Engine Optimization (SEO) is key to being found online
- Create business profiles on every related social proof platform
- Monitor review boards weekly, and respond immediately
- Focus social media efforts on one to two platforms your client uses, but have profiles for each
- Reviews and client referrals are the least expensive and most influential marketing
- When responding to review, keep it professional whether you agree or not
- Ask for referrals, and make it easy for clients to submit review
- Consistent content across profiles and platform increase link-abilty

Chapter 7: Marketing Strategies

Why did you choose the piano bar? Surely there is a reason you go to and frequent the places you do and buy the things you buy. You didn't know you were going to meet your significant other, yet you did? You went because you like live music, the pricing is within your budget but most importantly you expect to meet or associate with likeminded individuals. You could have gone to a pub, a hole in the wall or a hotel lobby bar. You went to the piano bar because they had the highest concentration of clientele you want to be around.

You've established a brand, logo, slogan, built a lean website and registered your business throughout the digital world via profiles and social media. You may be getting new client leads already, or at least hopefully. Once you establish your presence, there are seemingly endless marketing programs, strategies and "fool proof" campaigns. All of them work in one way or another but not necessarily for every business type. Yard signs may be great for landscapers and home improvement services, but not so much for an accountant or web designer. When considering a marketing product, service, or potential strategy the key is return on investment (ROI) both monetarily and time. This section focuses on marketing materials, strategies, avenues and lead generation.

Once you open shop and people know or see you, the B2B sales agents, charities, and experts come knocking and calling. Fighting off other salespeople when you are trying to sell something is frustrating, but it could be worse—no one calls you. If no-one calls you, that means they don't even know about you, so chances are customers don't either.

Every marketing campaign *should* have a central goal with KPI's to  determine if it's working. Any marketing or advertising campaign you don't or can't measure is a waste of time and money. The primary goals of most marketing campaigns are three tiered with brand recognition, increasing market share, and transactional direct measurable sales or conversions.

In simple terms:

- Increase brand awareness—tell people who you are.
- Marketing a new product or service—inform people who know or may have heard of you about a new outfit.
- Advertise something to influence people to act (or buy something)

The measurements (KPI's) are:

- Reach: how many people CAN see what you're showing.
- Impressions: how many people DO see what your show.
- Conversion: how many people see and ACT on what you showed.

The strategy is how and what you will do or use to accomplish each goal, and how to measure it.

- **EXAMPLE:** Expanding on an earlier example: Think of a commercial that has animated polar bears in red and white, what beverage are they drinking? You may see another commercial not long after with the slogan "same great taste, without the calories". The next commercial break may say, "12 pack of X $3.99 at your local grocery store this weekend!" The polar bears job was to remind you that you trust the brand. A million people may watch that channel on average per day (reach). Of those million, 100k had the TV on and saw the commercial (impressions). 1,000 went to the grocery store and bought soda that weekend (conversions).

Since the possibilities for brand recognition, market share and advertising are ostensibly endless the focus for now is fundamentals for simplifying, tracking, sourcing and converting. Most strategies fall in to one or a combination of these categories: Person to Person, Tangible and Print, Digital and Social. There are Pros and Cons with each category which will be discussed in  detail. Regardless of the strategy, the tradeoffs are time vs money, but also reputation and confidence.

Most new business have limited marketing and advertising budgets, so they try to do all three with one ad. Before you invest time and money on a strategy, develop the goal and how you will measure it. The easiest way for a new business to determine what strategy is working is to simply ask a new lead or customer, "How did you hear about us"? If you don't ask, know or have some sort of way to identify  how or what led the customer to you, the time or money invested is going right down the drain.

Goals

1. What is your goal:
    a. Branding, or introducing yourself to new people?
    b. Market Share reminding people of why you?
    c. Advertising, or selling a specific product or service?
2. Where or what's your target market or area?
    a. Introduce yourself to an existing or new area
    b. Covert or bring new people into your brand
    c. Sell a specific product or service in an area
3. How will you measure success?
    a. Reach and Impressions
    b. Impressions and conversions
    c. Conversions and sales

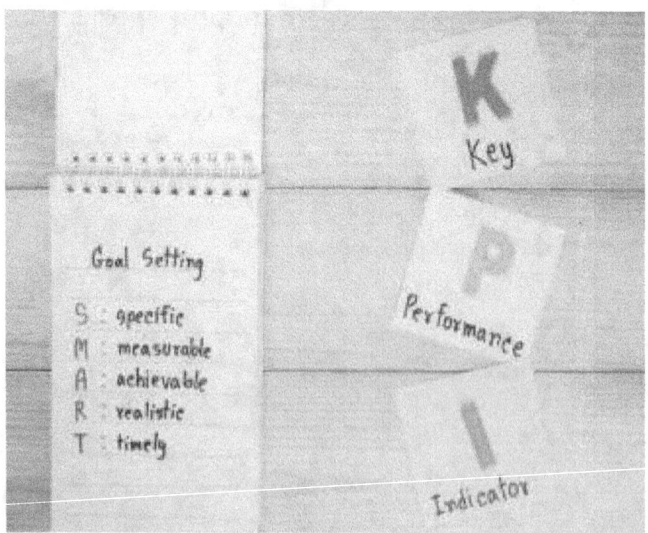

Active or Passive Strategy

Once you identify the goal, area, and how it will be measured the next aspect is your strategy. Are you actively engaging or passive waiting—meaning; are you going out and knocking on doors and handing out business cards, or putting a sign up, wrapping your car and waiting? The scope will determine the cost both time and money. A passive strategy often reaches more people in less time, though their interest level may be limited. An active strategy can reach the right people for a limited time, but less overall. Let's start with person to person, which is an active strategy with a short reach, but the highest conversion. The primary cost is TIME.

Person to Person

Person to person marketing and advertising is one of the oldest forms of active marketing and sales. In the digital age, it is rarely done due to the time commitment required, and limited reach. However, person to person marketing and sales has the highest conversion and repeat business rate. Person to person marketing often leads to customers for life because you put a face on a product or service and clients feel connected, valued and special. The key question to ask yourself is do you want a customer for life, or a customer for a day. Examples of person to person marketing are as follows.

Pied Piper

When Robert Browning wrote the Pied Piper of Hamlin, he probably didn't think it would become a central theme in business marketing and advertising. Pied Pipers are social influencers, bloggers, and famous people who consciously and subconscious play a key role in buying habits. Whether it's a retired athlete or hot new movie star, they may tell you about cheap car insurance and you buy it even if the stars haven't touched a dollar bill in years. Unless you have a BFF that's rich and famous, you may need to start smaller.

You probably know a few small-time influencers in your social circle,

 maybe your best friend, mom or religious leader talks to every single person they see. Even if they only have a few hundred followers, if they are active followers that's a few hundred people you can potentially reach if you talk to them and

they believe in your product or service. People you don't know can be pied pipers too if you know where to look. Maybe you know a chatty secretary at your doctor's office, or your local cashier at the grocery store. These people are front line all day every day making small talk with strangers. Do they have your business cards and think you provide a great service? Depending on what you do, a I Love XYZ business sticker, pin, button, or T-shirt could turn that small talk in to customers for you. Maybe a $5 amazon gift card can influence them to turn the small talk in to customers for you. Consider the ROI though, if you only earn $5 per sale, it may not be worth it.

Canvassing

Good old-fashioned canvassing. Canvassing is walking around your target area and knocking on doors. Some areas and neighborhoods have a prohibition on traditional canvassing, but people still do it. Depending on your business type, canvassing can work wonders. In lieu of direct mail (discussed later), you can have postcards and flyers made specific for your business and go door to door. A web designer, travel agent or law firm probably wouldn't do well, but if you provide a mobile service especially that's recurring you can build a base of trust and a client base over a couple weekends.

- **EXAMPLE:** If you are a landscaper, handyman, general contractor, pet sitter or walker, auto detailer, mobile barber, hairdresser, nail salon, childcare, or organizer you are putting a name and face directly in front of someone who may be interested.

Post pandemic, people want and need personal services at home. If you specialize in children's haircuts, walking around a neighborhood looking for a swing sets in the back yard is a great start. Look professional, have a larger flyer with credentials and just introduce yourself. If you're a roofer or landscaper, how does the roof and yard look? Stop by and say: "Hi neighbor, I live down the street and cut most of OUR neighbors' grass if you're ever too busy to do it" and hand them a flyer. Canvassing can pick up multiple clients in a targeted area over a couple weekends. With canvassing your reach will be low, but your impressions and conversions will high. If they aren't interested, ask them if they know anyone who is and get contact details for your CRM. If you have time and want to build

good will and a reputation– assuming it only costs time, offer to come back or do it free as a 'free trial'--but ASK FOR A GOOD REVIEW! "If you want, I can cut your lawn real quick right now" and put out a yard sign. It may have cost you a half hour, but every neighbor sees the sign, and you now have some social proof.

Sidewalk Sales, Charities, Fairs, Trade Shows

If you want more public exposure and social proof—rent a booth. Many towns and counties, as well as industries have pop-up events to advertise and sell your wares as well as check out the competition. Main street sidewalk sales, carnivals and non-profits frequently look for sponsors and small businesses to rent space at their event. If you don't want people coming to your house or place of work a small booth for a couple days will help you get the word out and put a face to a name. You may bump into a neighbor who's only a block away and had no idea you were a bookkeeper as a side gig. Sidewalk sales, fairs and non-profit don't charge much to set up a table for a day or two.

Trade shows are often multi-day and may break the bank. That doesn't keep it out of reach though if you're savvy. Maybe you can piggyback on another vendors booth, or cost share with a complimentary business. If you're a plumber, split the booth with a roofer, or swap days with a couple other local small businesses.

Often the idea of a sidewalk sale doesn't make sense for service providers since they don't have tangible products to sell, and the cost both time and money doesn't immediately affect your bottom line. However, they are an excellent opportunity to brand and market with promotional items, hand out flyers and build a client database. If you decide to participate in a sidewalk sale or otherwise there are multiple ways to attract people to your booth.

Many companies offer games of chance, to 'win' a free something. New roof, bathroom, car, home remodel or vacation. You may think you can't afford to buy or pay for the prize if someone wins but you don't have to. You simply purchase an insurance policy for the cost, and should someone win you got a new client and a huge sale paid for by the insurance policy.

- **EXAMPLE:** A roofer may offer to replace a roof if you roll the dice and spell their company name. If a customer wins, your insurance policy will pay you the $20k for the new roof.

If you decide to go the route of a pop-up, trade show or otherwise you'll want to clearly identify your objective, which for service businesses is typically lead generation, branding and marketing.

Best Practices:

If you intend on doing person to person marketing, purchase or have a branded uniform, polo shirt or something that identifies you as the vendor. Name tags work, but you may want something with your brand, logo, color's and slogan. Giveaway or promotional items also put your brand, logo and preferred contact method directly in someone's hands. Inexpensive options are pens, note pads and calendars, and hand sanitizer which is a hot commodity right now. The more useful and relevant to your business, the better.

- **EXAMPLE:** A carpenter may want to give away carpenter pencils with their name, phone and logo on them. (Of course, if you made your logo multiple colors and it has tons of detail it won't fit on a pencil).

Business Cards

Business cards a print and tangible, however primarily used in person to person marketing. Take a look in your wallet or purse right now, maybe you have to fish through a junk drawer or your glove compartment. How many business cards do you have…*that are someone else's?* Many people rush out to buy business cards, it's one of the first tangible things that may represent your business. Often, they are a sense of pride and make you feel like you are on your way. However, you don't have any in your purse or wallet right now from someone else.

The reality is people don't keep business cards when you hand them out. If you give one away and the person takes a picture of it, or immediately adds the info in their phone they *may* call you. Business cards are social proof in a way, but more so for you. Have you ever looked at a business card and thought this card is of such high quality that I will surely give this person a call? Some business cards are odd shapes, different thicknesses, made of plastic or PVC which make them 'stand out'. As unique as they may be, if they don't fit in the standard business card sleeve or holder, people often just throw them away. Business cards are more for you, than for the people you give them to, especially in the digital age.

Business cards are tangible materials with a monetary cost $10 and up depending on quality, quantity, and whether you DIY or have someone design for you. If you DIY, remember what your time is worth before spending four hours designing them. Reach for business cards usually is the length of your arm, and often it's one person at a time. You can leave a stack of business cards in target areas, but will you check or track if they are taken or not, and replenish them at a scheduled date? Business cards are great to give to your Pied Pipers. You should have an associated source code for business cards AND codes if you plan on leaving them around town per location. Business cards can be both active and passive, but you think of your personal experience with them before committing too much time or money.

Tip for Business Cards

When the time comes, if you want to buy business cards the key is clarity and emphasizing a specific call to action. You have a logo, company name, slogan or tag line, web address, email and phone number. Make your preferred contact method BIGGER and bolder. The best business cards have the person's name, logo, and phone number on one side and sometimes their picture – simplicity is key. All the remaining contact information is on the back. Your business cards should blank space on the card so you can write something. The best practice for business cards is always have a handful with you. When you give them out ask the person for their contact number and write it on your card, along with where you met them and a quick note 'wants XYZ'. Give them a blank one and keep the one you wrote on to add in your CRM and call later. Now it doesn't matter if they call you or not, because you're going to call them and say, "Hey Joe, we met yesterday at the grocery store and chatted about XYZ". Keep in mind, older generations ask for and still use business cards, don't make your font microscopic or too busy with italics or other fancy text.

- **NOTE:** Many small businesses forgo business cards and use post cards instead. They are more recognizable, contain more content and have multiple uses to include all you would use a business card for. If you're canvassing, post cards are better than business cards.

Print and Tangible Marketing

Direct mail, whether postcard, letters, flyers or magazines is a relatively easy way to contact and reach specific individuals within your target market. Direct mail saves time, but costs money. Your post office provides this service along with many other resellers, printers, and advertising companies. The benefit of direct mail is you can target and reach new customers based off their demographic by creating a new list with public data or carrier routes.

Most companies and the post offices have tools for you to select who gets what marketing piece, or you can upload your own list. Direct mail is a good option if you are advertising a new product, service or sale. However, the reach is only as big as your budget because you typically pay per piece created and mailed. Direct mail is usually a one-off marketing piece and is valid for a shorter period of time. However, if you're designing it, it's possible to make the sale timeframe longer, but once someone sees and read it, they likely throw it away. Look at your fridge, do you have any direct mail on it with magnets? Direct mail costs vary depending on the level of service, size, weight and number of pieces. Usually the end cost is 40-80 cents per piece for a postcard or letter. Direct mail is a good option for marketing a service like hair salons, accountants, or anything that would require a schedule or blocking out time. Direct mail is also a great advertising option for sending promo codes, coupons, menu's and new product offering.

Direct mail works best for specific businesses and services. If you are offering a product or service 100% online, direct mail may not be the best route. Send them a 'digital' post card, or email instead.

Younger demographics often don't read mail and flyers, most of their mail goes to their parent's address, an old address, or they dread it because it's bills. The bulk of individuals under 30 don't respond to mailers. When they do respond, they likely go right back online to look it up and may just buy online from whoever offers it the cheapest. If you are under 30 and reading this, have you ever gotten a mailer and called the number on it right away?

Your reach is how many pieces you buy, your impressions are how many people open or see it, your conversion is how many contacts or leads you received from your mailer. If you don't add a source, promocode or ask your new leads and clients how they heard about you—again, you're wasting money.

- **Direct Mail Tip/Option:** Although slightly more expensive, one of the best direct mail pieces for small businesses is calendars. You can print, design and direct mail calendars, with 12 pictures of your business or service and recipients are less likely to throw them away.

Billboards and Car Wraps

Billboard and car wraps function the same way, just one is on wheels and directly advertises in your service area, or wherever you drive. If you deliver or do onsite work a vehicle wrap is one of the best options if you don't have a static or brick and mortar location. Both billboard and vehicle wraps are geared toward brand recognition and marketing, but not usually advertising because they are more permanent and expensive to change. Both billboard and car wraps are higher cost and longer commitment. Car wraps cost from $1200+ depending on your vehicle size and location. Billboards start at around $500 a month if you commit for a longer period.

Billboard placement and reach is determined by vehicles per day (VPD) or vehicles per month (VPM). The factors to consider with a billboard are not just reach, exposure and cost—placement is perhaps the most important. If you are a local business with specific service areas, a billboard on an interstate probably isn't the best choice. Sure, you may reach 500k+ vehicles per month, but if your product or service area is limited to your town, interstate exposure is worthless.

- **EXAMPLE:** A billboard on an interstate highway for a daycare or landscaper in town isn't likely going to make people traveling the coast stop and drop their kids off, and you probably won't drive hundreds of miles to cut someone's grass.

Placement is also important when considering competition. Advertising a small restaurant with a huge cheeseburger on a road or highway filled with competition may be counterproductive. If your business isn't on that highway, you may be making people hungry and they won't detour 30 minutes to get to you when another burger joint is up next on the left. On the contrary, it may be a great option if you're trying to bring people who intended on going to those burger joints to try you out.

Car wraps are the best option for small local businesses because they follow you. If someone is interested in a parking lot, you can talk to them immediately and present your value proposition. Additionally, whenever you drive, you're advertising and it's a great qualifier for your taxes if you are looking to claim your vehicle as business use.

Print Media

Newspapers, newsletters, magazines and your weekly coupon books are the were one of the greatest ways to market and advertise, yet most are moving digital. Advertising in print seems to be gradually fading away or the costs are increasing due to overhead expenses. Costs for print media advertising is calculated by placement and per column inch (PCI) or column centimeters (CC). Rates vary exponentially depending on the overall reach, and whether you want to be front, back or anywhere in between. Printed news, magazines and other mass distribution channels primarily have older demographics. So, if your ideal customer is older it may still be a good avenue to explore. Since nearly all print media has some sort of digital version or counterpart check on the reach and if it consists of both print and digital subscribers. If the pricing is calculated off a million subscribers, and you want to be in print – that may not mean a million print copies will be distributed.

One the other hand, editorials and newsletters can be a great option if you have time and patience. Often a story will be published for free if you invest time building relationships. Editorial content is anything published designed to inform, educate or entertain and is not created to attempt to sell something. Often if you are a new business, provide a unique or new product and service you may be able to contact editors and publishers to do a story on you and your business. As long as it's presented to educate or inform the public they may write, publish and print the story at no cost. If you present it or the article sounds like a sales pitch; it becomes advertising and they will likely try to sell space.

A new business opening in a small town often can be published as an editorial, with the story discussing the owner's location and story. If the story says 'we sell this for $10' it will be disqualified as commercial content. A great starting point to get in print with little to no costs is your chamber of commerce, library or local municipality. They often have weekly or monthly short newsletter printed and distributed locally and paid for

with donations and/or tax dollars. Editorials are often free print media, but must not advertise, and usually is a good informative story.

Commercials and Radio

Commercials and radio are one of the most expensive marketing strategies and are used for all three campaign aspects. Whether brand awareness, marketing or advertising they are effective if used on the right channel at the right times. The cost of TV commercials or radio ads varies based off reach, the number of times run, and the times they are run throughout the day. Your ideal customer has various behaviors and habits, so understanding when they watch TV or listen to the radio is the most important aspect to consider. It may be far less expensive to run an ad at midnight, but if your ideal customers are parents with teens, they may not be awake.

The station whether tv or radio has demographic groups overall and for specific times. Advertising diapers on the history channel would be less effective than on a kid's channel. Sure, kids don't buy their own diapers, but parents typically watch or listen when kids are in front of the TV. Advertising nationally often is far more expensive than a targeted audience or area. You can run an ad or commercial through your local tv provider or cable company that is in between a national shows or news. Meaning, if you watch CNN your commercial can run between their commercial breaks, but only local viewers and areas see it. This option is far less expensive than buying time for the whole state or country.

If you are using it to advertise, you should have unique source codes to track sales. "Call now and use PROMO CODE [AWESOME] for a special deal" You should have a different promo code per time slot to determine which ads and times have the best results.

B2B and Network Marketing

Business to business and network marketing takes more time than money. Network marketing often starts with friends and family who may be in business, but a central starting point is your local chamber of commerce. Most towns, counties and states have chambers of commerce, business associations, and business networking groups. The common goal of these groups is to support and promote local businesses within specific territories through shop small initiative or "small business Saturdays". Before engaging in a network marketing initiative, clearly define the time cost and have an exit strategy if you aren't getting a positive ROI. If your ideal customer is other businesses or B2B network marketing avenues are imperative. If your ideal customer is B2C, triple check your time requirement because often you are committing quite a bit with a low ROI or explore unconventional network marketing.

Chambers of Commerce usually have one time, annual, or monthly membership fees and dues depending on the size and area. Most chambers have regular schedules and meet 1-4 times per month. This is a great opportunity to meet, coordinate and work with other business owners in your area. The key to chamber meetings is bring value and business cards but focus on the value. Some chambers are very effective and have plans and ways for industries to connect and work together, while others are just owners and managers handing out business cards bragging about being masters of the universe. If you chamber doesn't provide value, local associates or specific networking groups may be a better option.

Business Associations often are a town or targeted zip code designed to help and coordinate activities in that town or zip code. Many require you or your business to be physically located within that territory. If your service area is multiple location including that town and you don't live there, they may not allow you to join. Non-residents or non-resident businesses can join, but ultimately there may be fees or a approval process. Most business associates have group pages on social media you can research and join.

Business Networking Groups or Initiatives (BNG/BNI) are less formal but often quite effective. Many business networking groups vote or allow new members based off industry. Networking groups often limit the number of individuals within an industry, and they are designed around a team.

- **EXAMPLE:** A networking group may have one realtor, accountant, plumber, lawyer and they schedule meet ups as needed at various locations. Many networking groups require a value contribution through presentations whether its market updates on their industry or useful information they group can use.

Unconventional network marketing or semi-formal networking groups, many opportunities exist if you ask and have time. Engaging another small business owner, or even a business where you're a customer is a great way to start if you don't want to commit money but have time. Creativity and win-win scenarios can lead to great opportunities.

EXAMPLES:

- Food delivery services, maybe your local eatery will drop your flyer in every delivery bag?
- A-Frame Signs: perhaps a local business with a storefront will put out a little sign for you?
- Shopping Center Kiosks: If you have a local mall and see a Kiosk, maybe they will sublease a shelf to you, and you can reward them with referral bonuses or a 'free' service. Maybe they will put out a A-Frame?
- New partner mass email and shared subscriber lists…which brings us to digital and social media.

Digital and Social Media

Digital advertising whether mass email, social media, blogging, boosted or sponsored posts is all about reach, impressions, and click through. In other words, open rate, likes, follows and subscribers. Digital advertising is one of the least expensive ways to reach the masses in a short period of time, and allows for easily measurable results.

There are dozens of companies that provide mass email services, and curated content to reach you're target customer. Some companies purchase, sell or rent email lists you use to reach new audiences. The CAN-SPAM Act is a United States law that regulates commercial email. While it doesn't actually prohibit someone from buying and selling email addresses, it does prohibit sending bulk unsolicited emails. If you're sending to a purchased email list, that's exactly what you're doing. If you purchase an email list, you are required to get consent to email from the recipient for marketing or advertising emails. Guidelines for mass email according to the CAN-SPAM act:

- Opting in
- Don't use false or misleading header information
- Don't use deceptive subject lines
- Identify the message as an ad
- Tell recipients where you're located
- Tell recipients how to opt out of receiving future email from you
- Honor opt-out requests promptly.

It may seem counterproductive to require opting in since the individuals and addresses have no idea who you are if you rented or bought a list. If individuals consistently mark your messages as SPAM you can be penelaized and fined. Even so, you can check your email and you probably have dozens of messages in your junk or spam folder right now. When you start small it's imperative to have a way or means to collect client or  potential client information and data if you want to reach the masses without paying. Mass email marketing companies ensure your messages and data meet the criteria to not be listed as SPAM initially, but if you're flagged you may never know.

Unconventional Mass Email

A good way to build a initial list is partner with a complimentary business. Meaning, what is your business, and what other businesses have similar demographics? Not competitors, they aren't likely to help you. If you're a barber, think hair salon. Even better if you're a hair salon, think nail salon. Plumber—Electrician. If you aren't competing with them and don't necessarily plan on expanding into their turf, they may mass email their contact list if you mass email yours. This is a win-win brand awareness and social proof strategy to get more people interested.

- **EXAMPLE:** "Jacks mobile Veterinarian is proud to announce our new friend Jill's dog walking service" or vice versa.

Ultimately, they mail their list, you mail yours about each other. Make sure you have a call to action or subscribe option, otherwise it would defeat the purpose. If you don't have social proof or have a bad reputation don't expect someone to email their list. Good lists take time to build, so if you SPAM or send irrelevant messages you may lose someone permanently.

Social Media

Many people start their marketing through social media, but often think 'reach' is the most important factor, or they advertise on the wrong platform for their ideal customer.

- **EXAMPLE:** If you're a home inspector in New York City, reaching people in New York state probably is a waste of time.

Just because there are millions of residents in New York, reaching everyone is expensive and unnecessary. Not everyone may own a home, or they do and have no need to get it inspected. Advertising home inspection services on Instagram or snap chat may be a waste because the bulk of those users are younger and aren't likely in the market to buy a house or can't afford one if they wanted to.

They question to ask yourself is, would you rather reach 10,000 random people with zero clicks, or 1000 with 100 clicks? 10,000 of course is more, but the conversion percentage is zero, yet the 1,000 had 10% click through.

When using social media as a marketing or advertising platform, be clear about who you're targeting and the goal. The goal may be to get more page followers, likes, or a specific call to action [CALL ME]. Likes and followers increase social proof, but that doesn't necessarily put money in your pocket right now. Having a friend recommend or share your ad often has a bigger impact then a random person clicking like. If all your 'likes' are from people who won't or can't buy, is it really doing any good? Look at your own personal account, how many pages to do follow, AND check regularly?

Social media marketing [PITFALL] If you have a clearly defined customer or service area, don't just create one mega ad covering everything and everyone. Create multiple ads with different criteria to gauge what is getting the best results.

- **EXAMPLE:** You will have better and more measurable results making three to six ads with a lower budget that are more specific than one huge ad with a higher budget. The first ad goal can before for followers, clicks and brand awareness, the second can have call to action buttons. Group them together as clusters of territories or post codes and age ranges.

SCENARIO: A accountant may want to announce a new business in their town and has a budget of $8 a day. The first ad goal may be for likes and social proof, and the demographics can be for a specific age range, income level and marital status and six zip codes. The second ad has the same goal, just six different zip codes, the third ad is the same goal, but for not-married people with a different income level. The fourth is also not married people, but different zip codes. The fifth is a call to action [request info] from the first set, sixth second set and so on equaling $1 a day each. After a week, what got the greatest results and click through? Re-tool the ad with what had the best results and run again with the best criteria and locations. Impressions and click through matters more than reach.

Look back at your ideal customer and start with their criteria. Putting things in perspective: 'Likes' and 'Follows' are brand recognition, 'comments' are marketing, 'clicks' are for advertising.

Videos

Videos are one of the biggest things people search for online and spend the most time actively engaged in. Whether it's how to, entertainment, or adult sites having a video that represents your business is a good idea. You don't need to be a pro videographer, unless that's your business and there are many free video makers available. A simple slide show of images, with voice over or music is a start, but anything with you or your team is more trustworthy and authentic.

Whether your business is sexy or not, the goal is presence and connecting with people. There are multiple types of video you can create not related to your product directly that show customers you are human. Of course, if you can create a video of you doing  your job with before and after that would work great and should be featured below the fold on your site. Make sure you #HASHTAG it.

Some video ideas that may be worth creating:

- You or customers reading reviews or video reviews of your business or service
- A happy holiday message from you
- 'It's our business anniversary'
- 'Thank you' messages to customers and clients
- A personal favorite: Thanksgiving messages "we are thankful to all our customers"
- Personal client recognition messages: ask for permission – usually clients are happy to and they will share it. This means more social proof.

Cold Calling

If you aren't asking for referrals, didn't create multiple business profiles, aren't getting reviews, don't want to market through social media, the mail, a booth event, partner with a complimentary business, or canvass—there is still hope, kind of. You can buy or rent leads and lists. Contact information and buying habits is big business. A call sheet or lead list isn't necessarily expensive, but a good one is. The best call sheets and lead lists aren't for sale, you rent them from the  owners. Cold calling works, but many people feel it's the original form of SPAM emails. Many phone services providers now mark cold calls as

[SCAM LIKELY].

Put yourself in a client's shoes; whether it's a legitimate call, scam or someone prospecting you probably don't want to answer the phone. If you've every answered a SCAM LIKELY call or have been called by a solicitor in the middle of your dinner, you probably weren't too enthused. If you buy a list, you get to be the person on the other end of the phone. Sound exciting? If this is the route you go, make sure you have a process and checklist of questions to ask when you get a live one on the line. Many list suppliers will also sell or provide you with auto-dialer software so you can make hundreds of calls an hour without typing each number manually.

Sponsored "Expert"

Depending on your industry, there are many consolidator and advertising websites. For a fee you can be a sponsored pro within various categories or buy inbound leads direct. You have probably heard of at least one of the big ones, but they are very common for real estate, home improvement, wedding

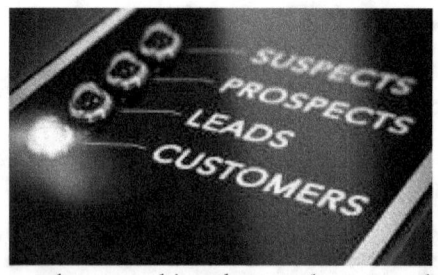 and bridal, and professional services like law and accounting. These programs allow for your profile to show up as a pro for specific services or specific areas, sometimes both. In Real Estate, you may show up next to a house you know nothing about or have no relationship whatsoever—but the visitor is none the wiser. Many offer the option to buy the next 'inbound lead' when someone requests information. You pay for that lead whether they make a purchase or not in most if not all cases. The fees can be per lead, per month, or a percentage of your sale. It all depends on what you sign up for.

- **EXAMPLE:** The bridal and wedding industry has many consolidators for photographers, DJ's, planners and sometimes jewelry, bridal shops or even honeymoon specialists.

If that's your business, check them out. But it may not be the best site for a landscaper or divorce attorney…but maybe?

- **EXAMPLE:** Trip advisor if you are a home-based travel agent. Close to half of trip advisor's revenue comes from Expedia (the DIY e-commerce travel site). Trip advisor owns multiple travel brands, rental companies and excursion services, if they own a company or property listed on their site would they say something bad about it?

Marketing Strategies Overall

Regardless of which marketing avenues you pursue, have a smart goal: specific, measurable, achievable, realistic and timely (S.M.A.R.T.). Start small and choose 2-3 areas you want to concentrate your time and money. Identify and measure what success, break even and failure look like before you invest any time or money. Be consistent with your marketing and brand. Create a line item for the cost both monetarily and time. Measure everything so you know if it's working or a waste. Most marketing and advertising initially will be a waste of time and money if you don't have social proof to back things up.

When you start small with a limited advertising budget, the more specific and targeted your campaign is the better. You can hunt with a shotgun or a sniper rifle, a shotgun can hit more and cover more area, but the sniper rifle is the kill shot. In less violent terms, is it more important to get sales in the beginning or let people know who you are? That depends on you and your goal, but if you don't have social proof or reviews from sales, even if you get the customer interested, they may not buy because no-one else has or the don't trust you yet.

- **BEST PRACTICE:** Focus on social proof first by going above and beyond to get good positive reviews. Focus on low to no cost leads through your lean website, business profiles, social proof sites, social media, business networking engagements, reviews and referrals. Most of these sources primarily require time, and limited money. Once you work out the kinks in your processes and plan, intruduce a SMART marketing strategy and work out from there.

- Create SMART goals
- Use multiple promotional or KPI's
- Use #Hashtags
- Choose the best strategy(s) for your budget and time
- Person to Person has the smallest reach but highest conversion
- Tangible Print can reach as many people as your budget allows
- Digital and Social are inexpensive, have a large reach but low conversion rate

Chapter 8: Money and Taxes

Engagement party, the rings, cost per plate the honeymoon and a down payment on the house—oh my. Who would have though meeting your soul mate could be so expensive? Many couples, just like businesses go into debt or burn through significant savings within the first year of their union. It takes at least two years to get back on track and pay off everything. Sadly, sometimes the union doesn't even last that long. However, you can fast track that payoff with businesses, and often carry over losses and deductions for years saving you a boatload on taxes in the long run.

Aside from being your own boss, creating your own schedule, and pursuing a passion most people become entrepreneurs to make money. It does take money to make money, but that doesn't mean you need to "take" it from your personal accounts.

Funding

Funding a new business usually starts with personal savings, loans, grants and venture capital. Most small businesses and entrepreneurs start by self-funding, or using money they procured through savings, retirement accounts or personal loans and credit. Day 1 is when you begin treating your business like a separate entity based off the corporate structure you created. Many businesses and entrepreneurs 'intermingle' funds within their business and personal accounts. This is perhaps the worst thing you can do because regardless of your business structure intermingling can and will remove the additional protection a corporate structure provides. If the 'corporate veil' is pierced, you can and will be held personally accountable for all debts and actions the entity takes.

Business Banking

The first step to remove yourself from liability is begin tracking and separating everything from your personal finances and business finances. Your business entity has an EIN, which as previously discussed is the social security number for your business. Once you create your corporation, open separate business bank account for your business using the EIN. If you are personally financing the business, obtaining personal loans from friends or family or intending on procuring a business loan, venture capital or otherwise deposit the funds directly in the business account.

- **EXAMPLE:** If you assess the initial expenses to start your business are $5,000 write a personal check to the business, and deposit it in the business account. If a friend or family member is loaning you money, have them write a check to the business—not you. You want a paper trail.

Opening a business account creating separation:

- Incorporate the business and get an EIN (personal funds)
- Open a business account with the EIN and fund it with a personal check: *MEMO personal loan to business*
- Write a business check to your personal account for the incorporation fees. *MEMO repay personal loan for incorporation fees*
    - *This will be your first business expense.*
- Once your business is generating a profit, write a business check back to your personal account for the amount you used to open it.
    - *MEMO repay personal loan used to open business account.*
- **TIP:** It is always a good idea to write the original check number or transaction number in the memo so you can easily find it if you need to.

Accepting or dispersing large amounts of cash may be construed as income by the IRS, and you certainly don't want to pay tax on it, nor would a friend or family member when you pay them back. **Note:** you can always claim it as a gift depending on the amount, but why complicate things?

It may not seem like a big deal when you first start because most of the initial expenses and minimal, but if the business doesn't work out down the road, keeping business assets separate from personal will ensure creditors can only target business assets. From now on, all business-related income should be deposited in your business account, and all business debt or bills should be paid from it. Simply taking cash out or paying personal expenses with business funds is the first  indicator you are intermingling funds. Even if the initial funds in the account were yours, you need to track and prove it is being paid back from an initial personal loan to the business.

If you rely on the business as a means to survive, or a primary source of income, pay yourself from the business and track it, then pay your bills from your personal account.

- **EXAMPLE:** Personal electric bill: Pay yourself from the business account to your personal account then pay your personal electric bill from your personal account. **[PITFALL]** Paying your personal electric bill from your business account.

Most accounting and invoicing software will allow you to add yourself as an employee or independent contractor. With this you can pay yourself from the business account and easily track it so tax time doesn't take hours of research. When you pay back the friend or family member, pay them back from the business account. This will protect you and them from the tax man if they suddenly receive a lump sum of cash and the government insists it's income.

- **EXAMPLE:** Check from Mom (#1001): $5,000 loan to business XYZ 1 January 2021. Business check to Mom a year later: Repayment of business loan received on 1 January 2021, check number 1001.

Since your business is new, and the EIN is new you likely don't have any business credit, and therefore a lender may not approve loans or offer a business credit card. Often if you need capital to start, you may have to personally guarantee a loan which ultimately puts you on the hook if the business can't pay it back. One of the best options for a small business to establish credit without personally guaranteeing a loan or line of credit is through a secured business credit card. Secured business credit cards work the same way as a secured personal card meaning you make a deposit for the amount of your credit limit and if you fail to pay, the bank simply keeps the deposit. If you are using personal funds, or procuring a loan from friends and family, this often is a great option to ensure you can pay them back. After the business responsibly pays the credit card over time, the bank will 'unsecure' it and return the deposit.

You don't necessarily need a business credit card when you first start. Using a personal credit card can be an option, however you are personally liable for the debt if the business fails. If you go this route, only use it for business expenses to ensure there are no co-mingling of funds.

- **EXAMPLE:** If you elect to use a personal credit card for business expenses, don't use the card for anything personal. When you need to make payments, pay yourself from the business account, then pay the credit card from your personal account. The personal card is used for tracking the business expenses and will be a neat easy statement at the end of the year.

- To keep things simple, whatever you intend on making as a payment to the card; pay exactly that amount. You'll still be on the hook for the debt since it's a personal account, however it will save a ton of time and headaches when tracking business expenses and tax write offs like interest down the road.

When you first start or open a business, you likely have some form of intermingling because there are associated fees with opening a business and that money comes from somewhere. The goal is to get your personal money and liabilities or guarantees out as fast as possible. If you go bust five years in and you used 10k of your own money, you can't simply sell the assets and pay yourself back then the other creditors. The assets will be disbursed evenly according to the law.

- **BEST PRACTICE:** Keep business and personal expenses as far apart as possible even if it takes additional steps.

Grants

You may have heard of scholarships or grants when it comes to students and education. Scholarship and grants are awarded to individuals for a variety of reasons, typically to aid an individual financially so they can obtain a better future and achieve their goals. Depending on who's in charge politically—the president, the senate, congress and even your local government, they have goals. If your business supports or aids in those goals, often there are incentives through taxes or grants available to support

them.

- **EXAMPLE:** If your new business will hire five new people, you may be provided with a tax credit per new hire if the political goal is to decrease unemployment. If the political goal is to decrease unemployment in specific demographics or communities, you may receive a higher credit depending on who your specifically hire, and where your business is located.

Aside from tax credits and deductions, the government often offers grants to support specific business types that support their specific goals.

- **EXAMPLE:** If the government goal is clean energy or renewable resources, they may offer a grant or lump sum of money to businesses and individuals who start or focus on providing clean energy.

The starting point is identifying your NAICS code as previously discussed. Search the web or the SBA discussed next at www.sba.gov for grants, or www.grants.gov. Alternatively, search the web for your NAICS code and grants to find additional non-governmental grants through private entities who may be interested in support your business type. There are multiple grants available not only for specific business types, but many for disenfranchised, minority groups, veterans, women and urban communities.

Business Loans and the SBA

Created in 1953, the U.S. Small Business Administration (SBA) helps small business owners and entrepreneurs pursue the American dream. The SBA is the only cabinet-level federal agency fully dedicated to small business and provides counseling, capital, and contracting expertise as the nation's only go-to resource and voice for small businesses. The SBA provides step by step guides on how to legally create your business, conduct market research, write business plans and proformas and assist with financing through approved lenders. The SBA was created to inform and help the little guy and main street.

If you sell hot dogs out of the back of your car and didn't take the steps to register your business, create a plan, and execute then don't expect the government to help. The SBA typically does not loan money. They secure

loans provided through preferred lenders and financial institutions. Many entrepreneurs rush to get started, don't cross the T's and dot the I's and then wonder why the SBA won't help or secured their business loan application. If you complete every step listed in this book, have it written down and the math makes sense the SBA is far more likely to give you the help you need. You may have to personally guarantee, may not get exactly what you ask for, but you'll likely get some assistance.

All lenders and SBA applications will need full and complete business plans and proforma to assess long term income projections. Before funding and guaranteeing a loan. Your first stop after this book should be the Small Business Associate (SBA). www.sba.gov

If you need help applying for an SBA loan, or grant see freelancers later in this book, or speak with a qualified accountant.

Venture Capital

Are you the next business pitching a product or service to Mark Cuban?

If a business loan isn't for you, or you simply can't get one. there are alternate sources to get started and raise money for your business or idea. The three main sources outside traditional lending are venture capital, angel investors and crowdfunding.

Venture capital or (VC) is a form of private equity and a type of financing that investors provide to startup companies and small businesses that are believed to have long-term growth potential. **Venture capital** generally comes from well-off investors, investment banks and any other financial institutions.

An angel investor AKA a private investor, or angel funder is a high-net-worth individual who provides financial backing for small startups or entrepreneurs, typically in exchange for ownership equity in the company. Often, angel investors are found among an entrepreneur's family and friends.

Crowdfunding is a way for people, businesses and charities to raise money. It works through individuals or organizations who invest in (or donate to) crowdfunding projects in return for a potential profit or reward. The most popular crowdfunding sites for business startups are www.kickstarter.com and www.indiegogo.com however there are dozens to search through and explore.

Budgeting

It's time to eat the hoagie, one bite at a time. Cost projections and proformas were briefly discussed earlier in the planning section of this book. When creating a business budget from scratch, or re-evaluating expenses it's easier to create a dream sheet for expenses leaving nothing out then decide what is a want vs need. Break business expenses down in to five key categories:

- Wages, salaries, and 1099 / freelancer expenses
- Licenses, permits, insurance, consumables
- Branding, Advertising and Marketing
- Software, Technology, UtilitiesRent/Mortgage, Equipment

W-2, 1099, Freelance

By far one of the biggest and most unpredictable expenses in business are the people. When you first start, you may be the sole owner or the only employee. Treat yourself like an employee or at least the manager and pay yourself a salary—consistently.

Down the road, you may find you need help and contemplate hiring someone or building a team. As a main street business, employees are one of the biggest expenses especially if and when minimum wages go up. The key

word is 'employees' because an employee is a W-2 registered staff member of your company.

Adding employees to an organization is expensive, time consuming and often a huge source of stress for a small business owner. You may be operating on a very tight budget, and if the government imposes mandatory minimum wages above the level of profit an employee can generate, you'll be stuck. Stuck because you can't expand or take any time off without bringing on a new team member, but the cost of a team member will not generate enough profit to cover their associated costs. So, the typical catch 22 scenario applies...dammed if you do, dammed if you don't.

First let's cover what an employee is, and their relative expenses. Employers are subject to various regulations, taxes, insurance and work conditions. First, employees are guaranteed a mandatory minimum wage. Depending on the state and federal regulations, you are required to pay this wage—for the sake of argument let's say $15 an hour. This is mandatory for every hour the employee is on the clock, regardless if they are working or generating profit for your company. Let's assume the employee works full time or 40hrs per week—2080 x $15hr = $31,800. This would be the gross salary you are required to pay, not counting additional taxes insurance and benefits like paid vacation or healthcare. You are required to pay employment taxes (federal and state) as well as OASDI (Medicare and social security). You may need a worker's compensation policy, unemployment insurance and will have other payroll expenses, timekeeping, tax prep and turnover should they quit, or you fire them. In the end, not counting turnover generally you're paying closer to $18hr or $37,440pa.

This often leads to many business owners to look for alternatives, cut hours or pay people 'under the table' which of course is illegal. Not only is it illegal, it's money or an expense you can't deduct when you file your taxes. So, the question is, do you need an employee? The answer is, maybe. You may be able to accomplish the same tasks with an independent contractor or

a freelancer—or perhaps an independent contractor or freelancer can accomplish some of YOUR tasks, and you can do the 'Employee' activities.

The IRS defines a worker as an employee or independent contractor based off control and the relationship.

Control. The relationship between a worker and a business is important. If the business controls what work is accomplished and directs how it is done, it exerts behavioral control. If the business directs or controls financial and certain relevant aspects of a worker's job, it exercises financial control. This includes:

- The extent of the worker's investment in the facilities or tools used in performing services
- The extent to which the worker makes his or her services available to the relevant market
- How the business pays the worker, and the extent to which the worker can realize a profit or incur a loss

Relationship. How the employer and worker perceive their relationship is also important for determining worker status. Key topics to think about include:

- Written contracts describing the relationship the parties intended to create
- Whether the business provides the worker with employee-type benefits, such as insurance, a pension plan, vacation or sick pay
- The permanency of the relationship, and
- The extent to which services performed by the worker are a key aspect of the regular business of the company
- The extent to which the worker has unreimbursed business expenses
- To determine whether a person is an employee or an independent contractor, the company weighs factors to identify the degree of control it has in the relationship with the person.
- Does the company control or have the right to control what the worker does and how the worker does the job?
- Does the company control the business aspects of the worker's job? These include arrangements like how the worker is paid, whether expenses are reimbursed, and who provides tools and supplies.
- Is there a written contract or employee benefits such as a pension plan, insurance, or vacation pay?

Will the relationship continue and is the work a key aspect of the business: Employees typically earn an hourly or salary rate whereas a contractor can be hourly, daily, weekly or a flat rate due when the contract expires and the work is done.

- **EXAMPLE:** If you are looking for help with different elements of your business like social media, advertising, answering phones, scheduling appointments, payroll, or anything that can be completed virtually with limited to no direction (because you gave them a checklist) a contractor may save you a ton in expenses.

1099 MISC/NEC

Independent Contractors (IC) or 1099 workers can perform tasks for a business as a contractor or subcontractor. IC's typically perform tasks autonomously and the employer does not dictate schedule or require reporting to predetermined locations to perform services. There is much grey area with the IRS and every case or scenario can be looked at independently. Independent contractors can be paid hourly (billable hours), flat fees per project based of predetermined tasks, or commissions.

Independent contractors are governed by a contract, or statement of work (SOW). The SOW indicates what work is to be performed with deliverables to receive compensation. Typically, if the work is not performed or no deliverables are satisfied the IC is not entitled to compensation.

It is critical that you, the employer, correctly determine whether the individuals providing services are employees or independent contractors. Generally, you must withhold income taxes, withhold and pay Social Security and Medicare taxes, and pay unemployment tax on wages paid to an **employee.** You do not generally have to withhold or pay any taxes on payments to independent contractors.

If you are unsure on whether a worker is an employee or an independent contractor, you can file and submit IRS form SS-8 for a determination.

Freelancer

The main difference between contractors and freelancers is that contractors typically work for one client at a time, whereas freelancers will generally work on multiple projects for more than one client. The amount that freelancers charge for their services will depend on their area and the work involved.

Freelancing has gained incredible popularity in recent years as side gigs or to earn extra cash. The scope and availability of freelancers has grown exponentially through various freelance websites and gig worker consolidators. As much as you may want to hire local and create jobs, freelancers often are a fraction of the cost and you dictate the terms of the contract and freelancers bid on the work. Ultimately you are auctioning tasks or work instead of a specific product. The rise in freelancers, like the rise in online shopping has diminished the need for brick-and-mortar businesses and many professional services. Websites like fiverr and Upwork offer a slew of professional services providers who take on one off tasks, or recurring support through bid systems.

Depending on your business, you may choose to simply sign up and become a freelancer or hire freelancers to complete tasks in lieu of hiring an employee. If your business idea is simply a gig service, you may choose to not start a business and just freelance until you have a client base to turn it in to a full-time job.

Hiring vs Freelancing Proforma

Putting things in perspective. Hiring an employee to create content, marketing and posts for social media and your website at $15 an hour for full time work as previously discuss had an annual expense of approximately $37,440. If your expectations for this individual are five 2,000-word content articles and five corresponding social posts per week, ultimately you could add that to a statement of work and bid it out to a freelancer. You may even find someone with more relevant experience on the topics you want the content on, and you could offer a fraction of the overall costs.

- **EXAMPLE:** $1000 a month for 20 articles and 20 content posts. The independent contractor would or could invoice you when the work is completed and performed. *Note: this is a high estimate for content writing, posting this rate you'd likely get hundreds of applicants in minutes.*

Sites like Fiverr and Upwork have social media virtual assistants, content creators, graphic artists, designers and many other professionals who can be retained on a cost per contract they bid on.

Nearly every task not requiring hands on or physical labor to be performed at a location can be subcontracted out to an independent contractor or freelancer. These sites allow you to create projects and tasks for freelancers and contractors to bid on and you are the employer select from the freelancers based off your requirements and faith that the project will be completed effective and efficiently. You can limit or modify scope of your project based off regions of the world, countries, pricing, experience levels and previous job performance as needed. If you have a particularly busy season, you could retain an IC or freelancer for only those months, or on a month to month basis without worrying about letting them go and paying unemployment insurance.

When to Contract

When you own a business, you may love or hate freelancers. When you're a freelancer the feelings toward businesses are mutual. Using a business or a freelancer comes down to you the owner and what your goals and budget are. Many small businesses rely on their local community as customers and B2B partnerships. Using a freelancer often is a one-off task or purchase, so service after sale is generally limited. Do you want or need service after sale?

- **EXAMPLE:** You may elect to hire a local design firm to create your logo and letterhead. Typically design firms have overhead, and if they are brick and mortar, they may have staff (W-2) designers. Fees for a logo and letterhead through a firm are either flat rate for your project, or hourly depending on the complexity. Many design firms charge $50 to $200 to design a logo with up to four revisions. New to the market or budding graphic design freelancers usually charge less than $10 with unlimited revisions if your post internationally. If you ask, or include letterhead design requirements they usually will throw those in.

The design firm may hold your hand and explain why they made a design a certain way, and if you are paying $200+ they may have (or should have) a target demographic focus group who voted on what they liked best. If you are looking for service after sale, like creating flyers, marketing campaigns or even printing business cards a firm may be a better option. If you intend on hiring additional freelancers down the road or searching and using a mass market printer-then the design firm may be out of your budget.

W-2, 1099, FREELANCER TYPICAL EXPENSES:

W-2:

- Pay rate, hourly or salary
- Federal Taxes
- State Taxes
- Medicare and Medicaid Expenses
- Social Security
- Health benefits
- Paid time off
- Unemployment insurance

- Workers compensation
- Recruiting fees (costs to post a job opening)
- Onboarding Fees
- Payroll processing fees
- Tax preparation fees (issuing W-2's
- Turnover expenses

Contractor:

- Contract creation (Statement of Work)
- SS-8 Contractor determination form (IRS)
- Salary, hourly commission or flat rate per project or contract
- Payroll processing or direct deposit fees
- 1099 Prep fee

Freelancer:

- Project Description
- Flat Rate or hourly per project
- Expense is tracked to bid system and credit card payments

Licenses, Permits, Insurance

Many businesses often don't add or calculate small costs that are required when they make their initial budget. You've already paid your incorporation fees; is there a renewal fee or associated license you need as well?

- **EXAMPLE:** If you sell insurance on a product or service, you may need an insurance producer license.

Many businesses, whether brick and mortar or home based are required to register locally on top of with the state. Though a local business license may only be $25 a year, you still need to add it to your budget. Some states require a full approval hearing for physical locations where customers and client will visit. Zoning, land use, business permits all have fees and they

vary greatly state to state.

Regardless of where you operate, you likely need one or multiple insurance policies to cover the plethora of scenarios you may encounter. Aside from specific industry related insurance like optometrist, accountants, funeral director, the most common are:

- General Liability
- Professional liability insurance / E&O
- Commercial Property or vehicle insurance
- Workers' compensation insurance
- Data Breach
- Home-based businesses
- Product liability insurance
- Business interruption insurance
- Commercial umbrella

If you're restarting, or have an existing business now is the time to bid out and update your business insurance. Most policies are calculate based off income and revenue, so if 2020 resulted in lower income you should look into policy refunds and reductions. Not every business will need each or any of these policies, so we will cover their purpose with a general overview. You can always check your industry type and NAICS code to find out what most businesses have, so you can narrow down your search.

General Liability

General liability insurance, also known as commercial general liability insurance or business liability insurance, helps cover: Costs for property damage claims against your business. Medical expenses if someone gets injured at your company. Advertising injury claims against your business.
Note: If you work from home, you likely get the same or similar coverage with your homeowners or renters policy.

Professional Liability Insurance / E&O

Professional liability insurance, sometime referred to as Errors and Omissions (E&O) is coverage for businesses that protect against claims from clients and customers. PL insurance commonly covers negligence, copyright infringement, personal injury, and more. This can include damages caused by things you did and/or things that you should have done. **Note:** Consultant, advisors, and professional councilors often require E&O

Commercial Property or Vehicle Insurance

Commercial property insurance protects commercial property from such perils as fire, theft, and natural disaster. It's generally bundled together with other forms of insurance, such as commercial general liability insurance.

Note: Again, if you operate from home, you may not need commercial property insurance.

Workers' Compensation Insurance

Workers' compensation insurance is a type of business insurance that provides benefits to employees who suffer work-related injuries or illnesses. Specifically, this insurance helps pay for medical care, wages from lost work time and more. **Note:** if you don't have employees, you won't need workers comp unless you want to insure yourself.

Data Breach

Data breach insurance is a type of monetary coverage purchased by organizations to protect financial interests in the event of data loss. Data breach coverage is a type of cyber security insurance (also known as cyber liability coverage) meant specifically for situations in which data is lost or stolen. **Note:** Many CRM, E-commerce, and hosted platform provide additional or ad-on data breach coverage

Home-Based Businesses

Home business insurance is a type of business insurance designed specifically for people who conduct their business from their home. It can provide cover where a standard home or business insurance policy might fall short. **Note:** Home Based Business insurance is a stopgap for business activities not covered by a homeowner or renter policy. It's is optional for most industries

Product Liability Insurance

Product liability insurance covers when a product or service you made or sold cause damage to the recipients. Typically damages someone's property, causes a bodily injury, makes someone sick, causes wrongful death. **Note:** General contractors, plumbers and tradesman often insure or bond their work and services. Additionally, this is similar to the 'small part' warning on children's toys as a choking hazard.

Business Interruption Insurance

One coverage most business owners need is business interruption insurance, aka business income insurance, and/or contingent business interruption coverage. It can help replace income you lose if you can't open temporarily after a covered loss, like property damage. **Note:** There are many ongoing lawsuits with insurance companies to determine if policies should or will cover losses due to COVID-19.

Commercial Umbrella

A commercial umbrella policy increases your liability coverage to provide payout for lawsuits that exceed your other policy maximum coverages. This type of insurance can feasibly protect your company from any liability claim, including libel, reputational damage, vehicular accidents, product liability, or customer injury.

Permits Licenses Insurance Checklist:

- State Incorporation Fees
- State Renewal Fees
- State Business License
- Township or Locality Business License
- Home Based Office License or registration fee
- Insurance Provider License
- Insurance Producer License
- Association fees, chamber of commerce, BNI
- Job or professional licenses, like real estate
- Lobbyist or union fees like ASTA or CLIA for Travel Agents
- Food service and Health code like grease trap inspection for food
- Fire and building code inspection
- Township, county or state approvals for commercial districts (zoning)
- Any or all of the above insurance policies specific to your business

Budgeting Branding, Advertising and Marketing (Bam)

Many branding, marketing and advertising campaigns and solutions are often one-time fees. Whether you're considering a placemat in a diner, a local newsletter, or boosting your social media pages divide it into a monthly cost and calculate time. If you pay $300 a year to be a member of your local chamber, and you spend four hours a month including commute time for the meetings what is your time worth--$15hr?

- **EXAMPLE:** Your line item in your budget should be $300 / 12 + $60 a month, or $85 a month.

Sure, $300 to be a member of your chamber per year may not seem like a big expense in the grand scheme, but do they market or advertise for that fee or simply list you and your company as a member? If they don't, and you can't commit the four hours a month to get and keep the word out there then why waste $300 in the first place? Think about your schedule, when do you want to stop, slow down, or do less hours per month? Will your manager go to those meetings on your behalf for free when the time comes? What ROI are you hoping for or projecting? $300pa +$60mo = $1020 annually, if you want a minimum or modest 2:1 ROI ($2 earned for every $1 spend) does your membership with the Chamber earn $2040 a year, and can you directly source sales to the chamber?

BAM budget and expenses can quickly and easily run away from you. If what you're doing isn't measured tracked and budgeted monthly, then it's difficult to add, change or justify expenses. If the strategy is set it and forget it, then the time factor is significantly reduced. However, if you aren't tracking and measuring effectiveness and earmarking monthly, next year you may not have the funds to keep it going.

Create a list of everything you would like to do, line item the time commitment for each and any tangible expenses or one-time fees. Once you have your dream sheet of BAM strategies, stick with the rule of three and chose which strategies have the highest ROI. Define a time and KPI's to review them, 30, 60 90 days, or perhaps 12 months. If the strategy breaks even after that timeframe, choose to modify, drop or expand in it for another timeframe. Anything with a negative ROI can be dropped or put on the back burner until the other strategies are generating profit.

Some strategies may have a zero cost monetarily, but if they are time intensive or require a hour a day, again look back at what you pay yourself or the future manager and your schedule—if this is a side gig, you may not have a hour a day available. If you do, or want to make time—what will you give up doing to free up this time?

BAM Checklist

- Time (every aspect of BAM will require time)
    - Pied Piper, Canvassing
    - Trade show, street sale, carnival, charity even
- Business Cards

- Print direct mail
  - Post Cards, letters, magazines, calendars
- Print consolidator
  - Newspaper, magazine, flyers, diner placemats
  - Editorials
- Print Tangible
  - Billboard, car wrap, signage, posters, window scrim
- Network Marketing
  - Chamber of commerce, business networking group
- Television or radio commercials
- Social media and boosting
- Direct or mass emailing
- Business profile site boosting or premium memberships
- Consolidator site preferred membership lead generation

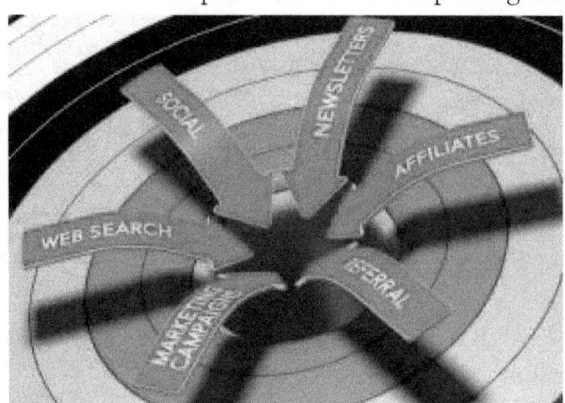

Software, Technology, Utilities, Consumables

There are a variety of software and automation systems available for small businesses, do you need one or multiple to accomplish your work? The most common systems for small businesses are CRM, invoicing, payroll, timekeeping, supply chain, lead generation, marketing and inventory management. Many businesses may have specialized software required for the job like bookkeeping. Purchasing the best of the best when it comes to software can cost upwards of $1000 a month, but do you need it?

Once you have your processes and checklists written down, how long does it take to complete each checklist? How frequent do you assess you will complete this checklist per month, and is it a key function that needs a personal touch? Although software programs will make running your business easier the question is will it save you

money or time? If a key process takes an hour to complete and you pay yourself $15hr, how many hours a month would the software system save you? If you only sell a handful of products or services per month, a full-fledged CRM may not be worth the cost when a simple excel sheet can accomplish the same tasks. Perhaps it's a key function you want a personal or customized spin on you calling customer after sale and asking for a review? What about invoicing and payment collection? If you do all invoicing manually and have to hand jam or type in what each product or service is, invoicing or automated systems may save you time.

- **EXAMPLE:** If it takes an hour to create, customize, and send an invoice then another 15 minutes to call and make sure they got it and pay, a standard basic invoicing system may be worth the investment. Most start at $10 a month, many only bill you if you send or accept payment. Nearly all invoicing systems will allow you to create a standard list of items or services which take out the manual entry and possibility of human error.

Keep in mind, invoicing and processing fees. If you accept credit and debit payments, usually there is a transaction fee and/or the system may keep a percentage of the sale. Of course, you may only accept cash or check, but most invoicing system will allow you to add manual or cash payments for free.

- **EXAMPLE:** Your invoicing system can track the client and payment with notes and instruction that indicate "sign here for terms and conditions and remit payment via ACH or mail a check to X".

Many payment and invoicing systems directly connect to your accounting and payroll for easy tax management. Square and QuickBooks are popular and relatively low cost. If you chose to purchase a software or CRM system to manage you clients and it's a annual fee, divide it to a monthly cost for your projection.

- **EXAMPLE:** $300 per year for a COTS CRM = $25 a month

Technology

You created a website, how much did that cost? It may have had a high one-time fee, but that probably isn't the end of it. You will likely have to pay for renewing your domain, hosting fees, and SEO if you want to stay on top. You don't necessarily have to pay for SEO, you can stay on top with consistent sponsored and boosted posts, but that will still require another line item. If you aren't contracting that work out or automating it budget more time plus the sponsor/boost costs.

Many businesses also look for and attempt to get vanity phone numbers or 800 services. With the digital age, and clients finding you on the web or clicking 'call now' often they aren't worth the cost because no one really dials the number or tries to remember the clever spelling of your business phone number. Think of the last time you called a service or business, did you manually type in the number or just hit a call now button on your phone? If you manually typed it, that business needs to update their website to make it easier for you.

- **Tip:** If you want a good easy to remember phone number, often you can get one with your area code through your cell phone provider if you have a dedicated phone line. Simply ask for a new number, then transfer or port it across.
- **EXAMPLE:** Your area code (###) 777-1234

Additionally, there are multiple voice over internet protocol (VOIP) and internet providers that will allow you to purchase a number and have it ring directly on your personal phone(s). This is a great option if you intend on hiring a virtual assistant because you can have it ring on their number while you're working, and vice versa. It's a great way to be open and available 24hrs even if you only personally take calls a couple hours a day.

Utilities

Utilities, heat air conditioning, water and sewer are predictable unpredictable expenses. Some utility companies have monthly recurring fees, others may bill your quarterly or annually. Always estimate high and divide the expenses up per month. If you have a low-cost month, don't spend the savings on something else—save and earmark it for a later bill. You may not use the air conditioning in April, but August the bill may triple. Utilities are expenses you can write off or deduct on taxes whether you operate a brick and mortar, or work from home. The way you deduct is slightly different for home, but the formulas are covered later in this chapter.

Consumables

Often an afterthought, but more in the forefront post pandemic. Consumables, not to be confused with COGS previously discussed are office supplies, cleaning materials, toilet paper to printer toner and copy paper. These little expenses often aren't calculated in a budget, but both cost time and money. Running out of paper towels and having a huge spill or mess may result in you or someone on your team running to the closest store to buy a few rolls. Sure, they may only cost $5, but if you're paying someone hourly at $15 an hour – your paper towels now cost $20.

- **EXAMPLE:** What if you have a large presentation to print and you run out of toner? The closest office supply store may print it for you…at 50 cents a page.

Many businesses will allow you to set up a recurring delivery for office supplies so you can set it and forget it. W.B. Mason and Amazon both offer this service and there are no delivery fees for the most part.

If you are creating a line item for direct deposit fees which is only a few dollars per person per month, why wouldn't you create a line item or process for consumables?

Rent, Mortgage, Equipment

Where you operate your business, whether home or a physical commercial location is usually one of the biggest expenses you have. Payments toward your location are deductible expenses, but how you deduct can be simple or slightly complicated if you want to maximize your deduction and value. Renting or leasing a physical commercial property is easy, whatever the payment is that's what you create the line item for. When creating and adding to your cost project, factor in any increases you may have

down the road.

Depreciation is the reduction in value of an asset over time, due to elements such as wear and tear. A car for example may get 30 miles to the gallon when new, but over time the gas mileage may decrease if you don't change the oil or do maintenance or get into an accident. In accounting, depreciation concerns allocating the cost of an asset over a period of time, usually its useful life. When your business purchases an asset, such as a piece of equipment, such large purchases can skewer the income statement confusingly. Instead of appearing as a sharp jump in the accounting books, this can be smoothed by expensing the asset over its useful life. Within a business in the U.S., depreciation expenses are tax-deductible. Owning property, whether a building or equipment will have a useful lifespan and can be depreciated over time. For commercial property the depreciation schedule is 39 years, while residential is 27.5. *(subject to change)* Equipment and/or furniture also has a useful lifespan and can be depreciated as well usually 3-15 years, but it depends on the equipment specifically. Simple depreciation calculators are available for free and allow you to compare the depreciation methods. **Note:** There are multiple depreciation methods depending on the asset contact a qualified accountant to determine what would be best for you.

Home Based Taxes

If you use part of your home for business, you may be able to deduct expenses for the business use of your home. The home office deduction is available for homeowners and renters and applies to all types of homes. These expenses may include mortgage interest, insurance, utilities, repairs, and depreciation.

The main requirements for home-based office deductions are exclusive and regular use. You must regularly use part of your home exclusively for conducting business.

- **EXAMPLE:** If you use an extra room to run your business, you can take a home office deduction for that extra room.

As of October 14th, 2020 the IRS Home office deduction requires you meet at least one of the following requirements:

- Exclusively and regularly as your principal place of business for your trade or business;

- Exclusively and regularly as a place where you meet and deal with your patients, clients, or customers in the normal course of your trade or business;
- A separate structure that's not attached to your home used exclusively and regularly in connection with your trade or business;
- On a regular basis for storage of inventory or product samples used in your trade or business of selling products at retail or wholesale
- For rental use; or as a daycare facility.

If the exclusive use requirement applies, you can't deduct business expenses for any part of your home that you use both for personal and business purposes.

- **EXAMPLE:** If you're an attorney and use the den of your home to write legal briefs AND for personal purposes, you may not deduct any business use of your home expenses. Further, under the principal place of business test, you must determine that your home is the principal place of your trade or business after considering where you perform your most important business activities and where you spend most of your business activity time, in order to deduct expenses for the business use of your home. A portion of your home may qualify as your principal place of business if you use it for the administrative or management activities of your trade or business and have no other fixed location where you conduct substantial administrative or management activities for that trade or business.

The bottom line: **You can claim a home office deduction if both of these apply:**

- You use your home exclusively and regularly for administrative or management activities of your trade or business, and
- There's no other fixed location where you conduct substantial administrative or management activities of your trade or business.

There are two deduction methods the IRS allows you to use; regular method and simplified. The three main differences are:

- Regular is a percentage calculation of your home and expenses whereas simplified allows for $5 per square foot up to 300sqft.
- The regular method will allow you to carry over losses where the

simplified method does not.

- Regular method allows for depreciation and recapture at the sale of the home, simplified does not.

Taxes

If you're new to business, or never really got involved in your taxes or the tax codes, business entities have deductions and credits just like a person. The tax code isn't designed to "get you" or steal your hard-earned money, it's a roadmap on what the government needs  help with. Nearly everything listed in this chapter is a write off or tax deduction. To be deductible, a business expense must be both ordinary and necessary. An ordinary expense is one that is common and accepted in your trade or business. A necessary expense is one that is helpful and appropriate

Before you invest time on a task, ask yourself if it is worth your time and will that task generate enough profit to cover your expense? If you time is worth $15hr and you spend 9 hours creating and updating your social media pages, did that time generate a minimum $225 of business income? You may work for free when you first start and open your business, but if you don't value your time you'll never stop.

SUMMARY

Below is a list of common business expenses and line items to consider. Multiple expense work sheets are simply by search small business expense worksheet online.

- Salaries, payments to independent contractors, TIME
- Consumables, paper, printer ink, postage, even trash bags
- Branding and Marketing: web site hosting, billboards, car wrap, signage
- Advertising: Flyers, mailers, social media boosting, lead generators
- Long Term equipment: larger purchases you depreciate over time.
- Technology, any software, bookkeeping or CRM (customer relationship management)
- Turnover: If you have staff or independent contractors, hiring, firing, recruitment
- Licenses, insurance, corporate renewals and permits
- Transportation and shipping, vehicle expenses, maintenance and fuel
- Taxes, state, federal, employment or OASDI
- Transaction fees, credit card or debit processing and consolidation
- *Utilities gas, electric, water, sewer
- *Communications, telephone, cell phone, fax, internet services
- *Rent, mortgage, storage unit

Chapter 9: Franchises

You tried and failed at the piano bar. You introduced yourself, you send drinks to people, and you been there every weekend for months on end. For whatever reason, you can't find the right person and the whole courtship ritual is exhausting. You know once you find that special someone, you can make it work, you just aren't good at first impressions. Franchises are like an arranged marriage. If you want to own a business but don't want to start from scratch franchising may be for you. Franchises are established brands, processes and systems. Most Franchises are turnkey business systems registered and regulated with the Federal Trade Commission (FTC). You may not be an expert in certain business aspects like marketing, accounting or branding, and maybe you don't want to be. The good news is most franchises do all the mundane tasks for you, or on your behalf. Your job is to run the business day to day using the franchise system. Most franchises are assigned a territory, region or postal code to service based off consumer demand.

Franchises typically have financial requirements to start, and a regular royalty or service fee structure to increase brand recognition, market and sometimes provide leads. Some franchises have quite steep liquid capital requirements, McDonalds is in the millions. However, many franchises are designed to work from home or independently and therefore have lower capital requirements (less than $20k). Many Franchisors offer preferred or in-house financing for the initial fees.

As with any business there are risks, but franchise systems generally are profitable and have proven models to generate income IF you follow the system.

Aside from the initial capital requirement, there are many factors to consider if you are thinking about purchasing a franchise. Perhaps the most important document is the Financial Disclosure Document (FDD). The purpose of the is to provide prospective franchisees with information about the franchisor, the franchise system and the agreements they will need to sign so that they can make an informed decision.

The Items Contained in a Franchise Disclosure Document

- **Item 1:** The franchisor and any parents, predecessors and affiliates. This section provides a description of the company and its history.
- **Item 2:** Business experience. This section provides biographical and professional information about the franchisors and its officers, directors, and executives.
- **Item 3:** Litigation. This section provides relevant current and past criminal and civil litigation for the franchisor and its management.
- **Item 4:** Bankruptcy. This section provides information about the franchisor and any management who have gone through a bankruptcy.
- **Item 5:** Initial fees. This section provides information about the initial fees and the range and factors that determine the amount of the fees.
- **Item 6:** Other fees. This item provides a description of all other recurring fees or payments that must be made.
- **Item 7:** Initial investment. This item is presented in table format and includes all the expenditures required by the franchisee to make to establish the franchise.
- **Item 8:** Restriction on sources of products and services. This section includes the restrictions that franchisor has established regarding the source of products or services.
- **Item 9:** Franchisee's obligations. This item provides a reference table that indicates where in the franchise agreement franchisees can find the obligations they have agreed to.
- **Item 10:** Financing. This item describes the terms and conditions of any financing arrangements offered by the franchisor.
- **Item 11:** Franchisor's Assistance, Advertising. Computer Systems and Training. This section describes the services that the franchisor will provide to the franchisee.
- **Item 12:** Territory. This section provides the description of any exclusive territory and whether territories will be modified.
- **Item 13:** Trademarks. This section provides information about the franchisor's trademarks, service and trade names.

- **Item 14:** Patents, copyrights and proprietary information. This section gives information about how the patents and copyrights can be used by the franchisee.

- **Item 15:** Obligation to participate in the actual operation of the franchise business. This section describes the obligation of the franchisee to participate in the actual operation of the business.

- **Item 16**: Restrictions on what the franchisee may sell. This section deals with any restrictions on the goods and services that the franchisee may offer its customers.

- **Item 17:** Renewal, termination, transfer, and dispute resolution. This section tells you when and whether your franchise can be renewed or terminated and what your rights and restrictions are when you have disagreements with your franchisor.

- **Item 18:** Public Figures. If the franchisor uses public figures (celebrities or public persons), the amount the person is paid is revealed in this section.

- **Item 19:** Financial Performance Representations. Here the franchisor is allowed, but not required, to provide information on unit financial performance.

- **Item 20:** Outlets and Franchisee Information. This section provides locations and contact information of existing franchises.

- **Item 21:** Financial statements. Audited financial statements for the past three years are included in this section.

- **Item 22:** Contracts. This item provides of all the agreements that the franchisee will be required to sign.

- **Item 23:** Receipts. Prospective franchisees are required to sign a receipt that they received the FDD.

The information provided in a FDD is clearly laid out, but key items to thoroughly scrutinize and understand before committing to a franchise.

1. Is the franchisor in good standing, have pending litigation, and their debt to asset ratio? If a franchise has limited to no cash or assets on hand but a massive amount of debt, it may be cause for concern.

2. The term of the agreement, and termination clauses. Many Franchises require a long-term commitment and/or non-compete clauses should you terminate your agreement. If you are unsure whether running a business is right for you, a long-term

commitment may require you pay fees for the duration whether you are working the business or not. This is financial commitment, so if you fail there may be legal consequences that may impact your personal credit.

3. If a service-based Franchise, does the Franchisor provide leads, and is there an additional fee?

    1. Some franchises provide a brand name, CRM and support staff, but you are responsible for building your client base. If you have limited to no experience in the industry, you may not have direct relationships with potential customers.

4. Does the franchise own any units or competitive brands that may undercut you as the franchisee?

    1. Some franchises own units or corporate operated branches you may find yourself competing with. Many brands use franchises as a separate revenue stream but provide direct to consumer products and services lower than what you as the franchisee can provide.

5. Royalty and fee structures: What exactly do you get and pay for joining and becoming a franchise owner? Initial fee and ongoing royalties are how the franchisor makes money and pays for whatever support staff they provide. Royalties range for 3-20+%. It is incredibly important to understand how and where the fees and percentages are calculated. Are fees or royalties based off gross sales, gross profit, net sales or otherwise? Are you required to pay a royalty or monthly fee whether you make sales or not? Are you paying a royalty amount on the profit per sale, or the gross receipt?

    1. If you are paying a royalty off a gross receipt, and the royalty amount is 10% yet the profit on the sale is 11%, your net may be 1% of the sale. Additionally, consider if royalties are capped annually, and what you would need to sell to exceed that cap. How many new owners meet or exceed the cap.

6. Lastly, how did you hear about the Franchise? Is the brand name well known in your area? Before searching for a franchise did you hear of the one you may be considering. If you never heard of them, maybe the brand doesn't have the recognition they are selling. If you heard of them because they are everywhere near you, are you

tapping into a customer base of territory already claimed and serviced by another Franchisee?

7. If a franchise is for a term agreement, ask to speak with new owners and owners nearing a renewal period. Review how many **paid** units added per year compared to lost units or individuals electing not to renew. You are working for yourself using their system, check social proof and reviews from Franchise owners.

The pros and cons of franchising depend on the individual short- and long-term goals.

PROS:

- Brand recognition. You are joining a team and organization who has an established brand
- Marketing: Many Franchises provide a website and marketing materials to franchisee
- Processes and checklists: franchises are business systems and provide established processes and checklists to contact, track, and follow up with customers.
- Training: Most Franchises provide training for their systems and processes as well as best practices based off trends.
- Support: Most Franchises have dedicated support networks and staff to assist new franchisees with building their business.

CONS:

- Initial fees: Franchises require initial fees for their system ranging from >10k to <1M.
- Royalties and ongoing fee structures: Some franchises have ongoing fees and royalties whether you sell or not.
- Term commitments: If you are new to business and join a franchise, you may be required to pay fees for the duration of your contract whether you work the system or not or have legal consequences.
- Marketing and Branding: You must use the marketing and branding provided by the Franchisor. Flexibility to do your own thing is often illegal and not permitted regardless if it works or not.
- Proprietary or non-compete clauses: Some franchises prohibit 'doing your own thing' after owning a franchise for set periods of time should you elect not to continue with the franchise when your agreement expires.

As with any business have an exit strategy and buyer beware. Some franchises not only survived but thrived through the pandemic. Others have been hit hard and may not recover for years due to regulations and guidelines outside their control. Understanding the business system, benefits, fee structures and owner requirements are keys to success in franchising.

Chapter 10: Getting Started

It's time to get started, and we will recap every section of this book with simple questions to move forward, provide general cost estimates, common pitfalls and mistakes and helpful resources you can independent research.

EXIT STRATEGY

1. How much time will you commit per day?
   - a. _____
2. How many days per year will your work?
   - a. _____
3. What is your time worth per hour?
   - a. _____
4. When will you add or decrease hours?
   - a. _____
5. When will you close down if it doesn't work?
   - a. _____

PLAN

1. What core products or services will you provide?
   - a. _____
   - b. _____

2. Who is it for?

    a. _____

    b. _____

3. Why do they need it, and how will it improve their life?

    a. _____

    b. _____

4. How will you tell them about it?

    a. _____

    b. _____

5. Who else does what you do?

    a. _____

    b. _____

    c. _____

6. How are you better?

    a. _____

    b. _____

    c. _____

7. Who will help you provide this product or service?

    a. _____

    b. _____

8. How much will it cost, and how much will you earn?

    a. _____

    b. _____

STRUCTURE

1. Who owns the company and has a stake in it?

    a. _____

    b. _____

2. How do you want to pay taxes?

    a. _____

    b. _____

PROCESSES

1. What key processes are needed for the business to function?

    a. _____

    b. _____

    c. _____

2. What checklists are needed to accomplish these processes?

    a. _____

    b. _____

<u>BAM</u>

1. What is your company name and website?

    a. _____

2. Describe your logo:

    a. _____

3. What is your slogan?

    a. _____

4. What is your one picture?

    a. _____

5. <u>In 50 words or less</u>, who are you, what do you do, and why should I care?

    a. _____

       _____

       _____

       _____

6. How will you Brand, Market and Advertise?

    a. _____

    b. _____

    c. _____

7. Where can new customers or clients find you?

    a. _____

    b. _____

    c. _____

<u>COMMUNICATIONS</u>

1. What technology or software do you need to communicate?

    a. _____

    b. _____

    c. _____

<u>HIRING</u>

1. What will you need the most help with?

    a. _____

    b. _____

Chronological Start-up Steps

- Write and fine tune your business plan
- Identify and draft the key characteristics of your ideal customer
- Find your NAICS identifier
- Register and incorporate your business
- Apply for and procure an EIN
- Open and fund a business account
- Purchase your web domain w/ business account
- Identify your service areas and/or procure a physical address
- Create a stencil simple website with company name, logo, slogan, one picture, and 50-word description & call to action button
- Register with business profiles: company name, logo, slogan, one picture, and 50-word description & call to action button
- Create a Google my business page: company name, logo, slogan, one picture, and 50-word description & call to action button request business address verification
- Update and add additional content to webpage
- DIY, hire or contract for initial SEO backlinking to profiles

- Create Social Media Profiles linking to primary website company name, logo, slogan, one picture, and 50-word description & call to action button
- Begin creating processes and checklists on how and when you will update your digital presence
- Create initial processes for common daily processes
- Create checklists for each process, including reviews and social proof.
- Create a digital and/or hard copy SOP for processes and checklists
- Invite friends and family to like and subscribe to your service web and pages
- Announce soft/grand opening (Chamber).
- Contact digital and print media editors and editorials to announce a new business in your area.
- Update your schedule with all partnership engagements
- Establish and schedule pop-up events if necessary, quarterly
- Schedule (BAM) component with KPI's for 90 days.
- SEO update

Typical Cost Estimates:

- Business account: free to $100mo
- Incorporating your business $25 - $800 plus time based off your state
- Employer Identification Number (EIN) $0
- NAICS code and registration $0

- Creating a business plan $20-$1000+ or $0 DIY
- Writing a proforma or cost estimate $20 - $500+ or $0 for DIY
- Logo design $5-$100, or $0 for DIY
- Web Address $1-$20+
- Hosted domain email, $5 each per month
  - (yourname@yourbusinessname.com)
- Web design $35 - $1000+ $0 for DIY
- Web Hosting: $10-$50 month
- SEO: $100-$1000+ per month to stay top choices (Flat fee initial linking and set up $150-300+) based of # of pages
- Business profiles at consolidator sites $0 for basic profile, $25+ for premium or sponsored (Flat fees $300+)
- Google my Business $0 but you will need G-suite or GMAIL
- Graphic design $10-$50+ per project, or hourly
- Bookkeeping: $10-$50 month for subscription DIY software, or $25-$150 hour for bookkeeper.
- Social media boost $1 per day per key demographic
- Video creation free to $200+ depending on complexity
- Explainer videos or white board: $50+ for 30 seconds

Best Practices and Tips Summary

1. Regardless of your entity structure, write down an exit strategy even

if you aren't required to.

2. Once you have a process or checklist written down practice it with a friend or family member to ensure it works.

3. If you put your logo on a coin, and dropped it on the ground can you see and understand the logo?

4. Call new leads immediately to introduce yourself and verify contact information. Leads unwilling to speak to you are far less likely to be interested in service and you can weed out fake leads.

5. When responding to good reviews add your #HASHTAG and mention your company name in the review if the client didn't.

6. When designing business cards, keep them simple. Print double sided with one side dedicate to a call to action. Name, Title, Image, Logo and Your preferred contact method. On the other side add all of your information streams like website, email address, social media handles, address, hours of operation, and whatever pertinent information you need. Your preferred contact method should be bigger and bolder than every other contact method. Leave blank space so you can write key pertinent information when necessary.

7. When you give out business cards, ask for their contact info and write it on a card along with what their interest is, when you met them and a key identifying feature. Give them a blank one and keep the one you wrote on to add in your CRM and call later.

8. Direct mail calendars are a great option for local business and have a 12-month shelf life. Although more expensive up front, your business stays front of mind for a year.

9. When funding a business account from personal sources, write checks and references in the memo for easy tracking at tax time.

10. Keep business and personal expenses as far apart as possible even if it takes additional steps.

11. 1-800 numbers typically are a waste of money for local businesses with limited service areas. Your mobile device provider can supply you with a good easy to remember number for minimal fees. (XXX) 333-1234

12. When person to person marketing, have branded clothing or marketing promotional products to build trust and confidence. Branded clothing can be purchases through multiple suppliers, one most cost effective is Queensboro.com, with no minimums.

PITFALLS TO AVOID

1. Unless every process is truly automated, don't be 'open' 24/7-365
2. Set a value on your time and stick to it.
3. Don't engage in tasks without a break even or positive ROI
4. Define what needs to happen to increase or decrease your time
5. Block out personal time for friends, family and yourself.
6. Pay yourself hourly or a base salary, NOT just keep the profits
7. Create a good entity that protects your personal assets.
8. Review your processes and model quarterly or upon introducing a new product or service. Review your plan annually and update it
9. Create KPI's for everything you do
10. Don't do something someone else can do for you cheaper
11. Cost out everything for your business and estimate high
12. Don't operate under the table, contract a freelancer.
13. Keep your logo simple and easy to understand when printed in black and white.
14. Don't get in to price wars with someone bigger than you.
15. Create a website for lead generation, not teach someone to DIY
16. Clearly separate personal and business funds and only pay or receive in the appropriate account.
17. Create all social proof sites with identical information
18. Create multiple small ads with different KPI's instead of a mega ad.

Final Checklist:

If you found any of the information contained in this work. Please review it on Amazon.

JASON BLOOMQUIST

NEAR ME

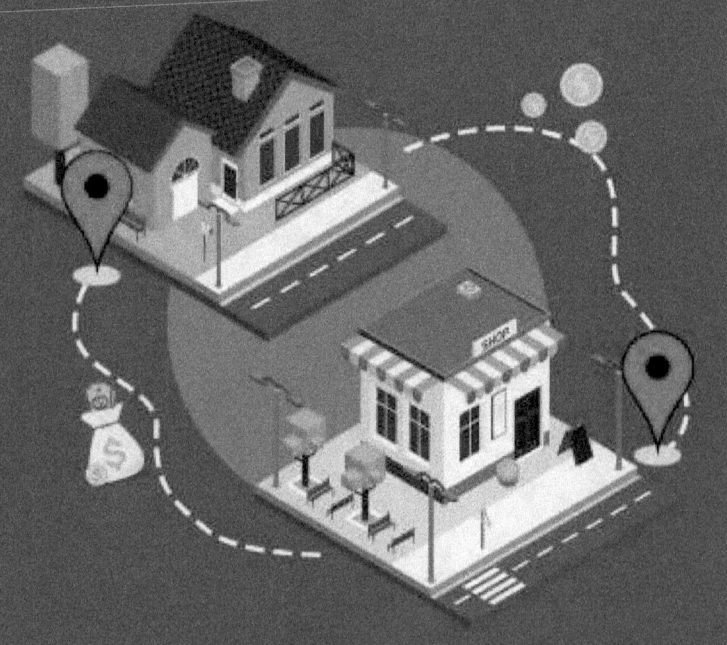

THE QUICK START GUIDE FOR MAIN STREET
AND HOME-BASED BUSINESSES.